MANAGING ANGER

Second Edition

Helen O'Neill, MSc, PGDip in CT, DipCOT
BABCP Accredited Cognitive Behavioural Therapist and Occupational Therapist
St Andrew's Hospital, Northampton

Illustrations by Clive Kemp and Michael Nixon

Whurr Publishers Ltd

The Atrium, Southern Gate,
Chichester, West Sussex PO19 8SQ
Telephone: (+44) 1243 779777
E-mail: cs-books@wiley.co.uk
Visit our Home Page on www.wiley.com

First published 1999 by
Whurr Publishers Ltd
19b Compton Terrace, London N1 2UN, England

British Library Cataloguing in Publication Data
A catalogue record for this book is available from the British Library.

ISBN: 1 86156 502 X

Printed and bound in the UK by TJ International Ltd,
Padstow, Cornwall.

This Manual is owned by:

. . . .

CONTENTS

FOREWORD

From the Stoics to the Victorians and to contemporary Western culture, there has been prominent societal interest in anger control. Now, the research literature in human development, personality, and clinical science buttress that broader agenda for the regulation of inner life. Far more than a matter of subjective distress and detrimental effects on personal relationships, deficits in anger control have been linked to physical health impairments and to the manifold harmful consequences of aggressive behavior. Humans are hard-wired for anger because of its survival functions. Anger is also part of the human fabric. There can be no sensible thoughts to negate it, much as the Stoics and the Victorians tried, but the aggression-producing, harm-doing capacity of anger is unmistakable, and so is its potential to adversely affect prudent thought, core relationships, work performance, and physical well-being.

Mental health professionals in many service delivery domains commonly encounter clients with anger problems and seek to improve their clinical care capacity in this regard, because providing services for people having recurrent anger problems is a challenging enterprise. Anger is a feature of a wide range of disorders. It is commonly observed in various personality, psychosomatic, and conduct disorders, in schizophrenia, in bipolar mood disorders, in organic brain disorders, in impulse control dysfunctions, and in a variety of conditions resulting from trauma. Anger management programmes abound, with dissemination in schools, clinics, hospitals, and prisons, especially of cognitive-behavior therapy (CBT) interventions, with varying degrees of systematization in implementation.

In contrast to amorphous approaches to anger management, Helen O'Neill's thoughtful and meticulous CBT programme is theoretically grounded and informed by extensive clinical application. It is primarily a treatment programme for people with cognitive impairment, as occurs with brain injury, and extends the stress inoculation approach to anger control for such clients in both group and individual therapy. It is proficient in its attention to the diverse needs of clients, it is thorough in format and therapeutic content, and her book provides many helpful supplements for working with clients.

The central characteristic of anger in the context of clinical problem conditions is that it is "dysregulated" – its activation, expression, and experience occurs without appropriate controls. Because anger is a common precursor of aggressive behavior, it can be unsettling for mental health professionals to engage as a treatment focus, regardless of its salience as a clinical need. Because seriously angry people tend to resist treatment, engaging them in the therapeutic enterprise is often hard going. As well, some people with aggressive behavior problems that are not a result of anger regulation deficits are inappropriately referred for anger treatment. Helen O'Neill smartly frames these opening issues and offers the clinician useful guidelines for safety, for evaluating the suitability of clients for anger therapy, for identifying clinical needs co-mingled with the anger control problem, and for deciding on individual versus group treatment.

People with serious anger problems are often ambivalent about earnestly engaging in treatment, largely due to the value that they ascribe to anger in dealing with life's adversities. The activation of anger may serve to engage aggression, perhaps to overcome fear, but in everyday contexts, anger is often maladaptive. Because of the instrumental value of anger and aggression, many clients do not readily recognize the personal costs that their anger routines incur; and because of the embeddedness of anger in longstanding psychological distress, there is inertia to overcome in motivating change efforts. Getting leverage for therapeutic change can be an elusive goal, particularly if the referral for anger treatment entails some element of coercion or if the person is reticent about engaging in treatment because he or she anticipates failure or abandonment.

Mental health and social services practitioners are thus in need of guidance in delivering interventions for people having problems with anger, beginning with the process of motivating clients to embrace the opportunity for therapeutic change and carrying through the regimen of treatment, which is often a painstaking and frustrative process. Helen O'Neill provides valuable direction for motivational interviewing, orientation to the treatment setting, and a 30-session treatment protocol, including a relapse prevention component. She also presents some wonderful additional sessions that build around prototypical anger scenarios, namely being told "no", being teased, being criticized, being on the receiving end of anger, and bearing a grudge. Her clinical sensitivity, inventiveness, and supportive style is evident throughout.

This marvelous book by Helen O'Neill offers many resources for treatment providers, including material and techniques to facilitate generalization out of the treatment room and to boost clients' self-regulatory skills, as in developing personal action plans and goal setting. She provides an abundance of workbook material that addresses the cognitive, behavioral and physiological domains of anger, including her own "on the spot arousal reduction" approach, and many well-crafted diary forms and worksheets. The cognitive-behavioral treatment of anger has been shown to have applicability to a wide range of client populations, and Helen O'Neill has pushed the envelope further in the service of clients with cognitive impairment. Her book provides a valuable contribution to the effort to help disenfranchised clients make significant gains in self-management and quality of social life.

Raymond W. Novaco
University of California, Irvine, USA

ACKNOWLEDGEMENTS

I would like, once again, to thank all the colleagues and clients who encouraged me to formalise my session plans and to produce the original form of this manual back in 1999. Special thanks are due to my two former Occupational Therapy colleagues. Firstly 'Creative Clive' for his updated drawings. Clive is now working with the Northgate and Prudhoe NHS Trust so I am particularly grateful for his continued support. I would also like to acknowledge Kirsty Pope whose interest and user feedback was a driving force to me. She was responsible for designing the signpost hand-out 'The assertive way'. This was created to illustrate an individual's choice of response and to clarify the meaning of some rather long words!

Thanks to all those who gave feedback on the first version, and I have tried to reflect this in the updated version. I am very pleased to say that this version of the manual also includes drawings from Michael Nixon, who was 'encouraged' to allow me to share his talents. Michael's drawings can be distinguished by the 'Significant slug signature'. He has also produced cartoons for the booklet *Managing anger after a brain injury* (2005) which I have written for **Headway** – the brain injury association.

Throughout the manual I have tried to reference the original source of material but some of the practical ideas have evolved from session materials acquired over the years, and their origins are not always clear! Therefore I cannot claim originality for all diaries and worksheets and apologise to any who may feel that their ideas are being reprinted as my own. Much of the graphic examples used have been developed during sessions both for, and with, clients.

Lastly, thanks to my family for their continued tolerance and willingness to share the computer!

THE PURPOSE OF THE MANUAL

This manual aims to provide a series of session plans to help the therapist lead a course of managing anger sessions with individuals who have 'cognitive impairment'. This term will be used during the course of the manual to refer to skill deficits or dysfunction, resulting from a developmental disability, acquired later in life following an illness or a brain injury, or long-term mental health problems.

Note: When studies are referred to, the terminology used in the particular study will be quoted: for example, learning disability, mental handicap, developmentally and emotionally disabled, or brain injured.

Why the manual was developed

The first edition of this treatment manual was published in 1999. It had evolved to fill a need as a practical resource to assist therapists working with individuals who have cognitive impairment. At this time the technique of managing problematic anger had become a widely used intervention in a variety of settings, including forensic, general mental health and non-clinical. Professor Ray Novaco of the University of California has been a major contributor to this work for a quarter of a century. He has developed a model of anger (Novaco 1994a), a stress inoculation procedure (Novaco 1993–4) for anger control, and an anger scale (Novaco 1988 and 2003).

The original work of Novaco and that of Feindler and Ecton (1986), who refined the principles for use with adolescents, was suitable for individuals of average intellectual ability. However, requests to treat individuals who had cognitive impairment had raised the question is cognitive-behavioural treatment appropriate for this population, and , if it is, then how could it be applied?

Attention was being given to answering these questions. In 1997 Kroese, Dagnan and Loumidis described the application of cognitive-behavioural treatment (CBT) for individuals with learning disabilities, and Black, Cullen and Novaco (1997) reviewed what little research had been carried out using anger management procedures with this group. Taylor and Novaco have since attempted to address the specific needs of offenders with developmental disabilities by designing an intensive individualised treatment protocol; and encouraging post-treatment gains are reported by Taylor, Novaco, Gillmer and Robertson (2004); (Taylor & Novaco 2005). Hence, the second edition of this manual both acknowledges these later works and includes further practical resources which I have developed whilst working with individuals who have an acquired brain injury.

Experience of working with such individuals has provided me with a challenge to tailor both the course content and the delivery of treatment to also suit this group. Many such clients have problems with intense anger arousal that seemingly occurs instantly. They may, of course, have any number of possible deficits in the areas of attention, memory, reasoning, executive function, problem-solving, perceptual or motor skills, and/or communication difficulties. Any of these may contribute to frustration and anger arousal, so it is important to be mindful of such difficulties when delivering treatment.

Environmental factors can affect a person's information processing. The severity of this became obvious only as I listened to clients describe the acute distress of escalating physiological arousal and angry cognitions that accompany their attempt to make sense of a situation in a noisy or busy environment.

This fits comfortably with Novaco's perspective that 'anger can be a stress reaction activated by exposure to environmental elements and conditions that are categorised as *stressors*' (Novaco 1994b). A person in the midst of acute stress experiences a reduction in their ability to make sense of a situation as their attempts to process information may become chaotic or ineffective. Fortunately, in most cases the stress passes and the function resumes, but for those clients with acquired brain injury it is not just a temporary state.

Hence my more recent work has provided me with a greater understanding of the complex process of anger arousal. As we analyse this process, to discover the sequence of events for the individual concerned, we realise that there are many opportunities for misinterpretations, misunderstandings and reactive responses. These can lead to the appraisal of anger in anybody, but if the individual involved has cognitive deficits or cognitive communication problems, then surely there may be additional potential for the sequence to go wrong.

The manual and treatment plans are not offered as an absolutely prescriptive programme. Material is presented so that each session could be followed literally; however because of clients' individualistic needs it is very likely that some amendments may need to be made. Therefore, each session offers pointers towards extra material that can be used either instead of, or as well as, the session plans.

Please note the title of Managing Anger rather than anger management. I feel the former highlights the treatment goal of developing self-management skills and consequently, having greater choice. The title anger management may suggest an external technique that is delivered to others. For the many clients who feel disempowered, the victims of blame and judgement, this can be an important factor when treatment is being suggested.

The development of this manual reflects both knowledge and experience gained in clinical practice, feedback from clients, and the influences of colleagues from occupational therapy, psychology, speech and language therapy and education departments.

Please note:

As we consider the literature on CBT, developmental disabilities, mental health and brain injury, there is scope for potential confusion about the use of the adjective 'cognitive' (O'Neill 2002). Hence when cognitive dysfunction occurs it could be as a result of an impairment of cognitive skills such as attention, memory, executive function and reasoning, or because of the interdependent cognitive products, processes and structures. We also know that when a person is in a state of emotional arousal their cognitive processing is generally less efficient. It is likely that our clients will have difficulties with many cognitive components.

BACKGROUND PRINCIPLES

THEORETICAL BACKGROUND

Anger is said to be the most talked about but least studied emotion (Novaco 1978). It would seem that anger affects the vast majority of people at times and that, when experienced, involves a combination of cognitive, physiological, behavioural and social components. As such, anger is just one of a cocktail of normal emotions that we are wired up to experience. At best it can energise, and give us a clear message that something is not right. This prompts us to communicate and/or problem solve; which may then give a sense of control or resolve. However, at worst it can be destructive and lead to an array of distressing consequences.

Until recently, if anger was studied, it was usually in conjunction with aggression or hostility rather than as an emotion in its own right. This may be because anger has no 'automatic status' as a clinical problem and does not have a formal classification in the Diagnostic and Statistical Manual of Mental Disorders IV (American Psychiatric Association 1994). It does, however, contribute to diagnoses such as post-traumatic stress disorder (PTSD), intermittent explosive disorder, antisocial, borderline and a number of other personality disorders (Siddle, Jones and Awenat 2003), and is implicated in a number of clinical disorders (Eckhardt and Deffenbacher 1995). These authors belong to a body of professionals who believe that there is reason to research anger and give attention to the related social and medical problems affecting society. They assert that, like anxiety and depression, anger can also present in severe and extreme forms. The likelihood of its becoming a problem, or dysfunction, increases with the intensity, frequency and duration of the anger, or when it leads to more frequent and severe consequences. Put another way, if the costs of the anger outweigh any activating benefits, it may well be a problem. Costs to the individual may be gradual, such as effects on physical health (McKay, Rogers and McKay 1989), or there may be immediate and obvious social costs following a direct behavioural response of angry aggression (Novaco and Taylor 2004, Hanks, Temkin, Machamer and Dikmen 1999).

Bernstein (2003) also considers the status of anger and writes: 'anger involves an almost hopeless intertwining of morality and psychology, yet our only hope for communicating effectively with angry people is being able to separate the two. The reason there is no diagnostic category for anger problems is that mental health people can't decide whether angry people are sick or just bad. Sick people are entitled to sympathy and treatment. Bad people deserve punishment. Grudgingly we insert *not guilty by reason of insanity* between the two, but that's for people who are really crazy. Where do we put people who are convinced they're fine, but whose actions drive everybody else crazy?' This question highlights the need to understand more about the individuals concerned, and the case conceptualisation.

Anger must be viewed contextually (Novaco 1993). We know that anger experience and expression is dependent on culture, upbringing and social support (Stevenson 1997, Tanaka-Matsumi 1995). Our culture, upbringing and beliefs may all influence what we label as anger and how we view it. It is sometimes seen on a continuum from miffed, annoyed, frustrated, irritated, cross, angry, furious, livid etc. and therefore semantics are relevant when delivering treatment. Eckman (2003) echoes this point, saying the word anger covers many different related experiences resulting in a range of angry feelings. Anger is rarely felt alone for long; for example fear often precedes or follows it. He goes on to say that anger is the most dangerous emotion and that angry people are not well liked. We will return to this point in therapeutic relationship.

Ellis, in Ellis and Tafrate (1997), regards anger as a negative emotion that can be both appropriate or inappropriate and Dryden (2000) has made the distinction between healthy versus unhealthy anger. This unhealthy or dysfunctional anger is probably the most frequent reason why a client is referred for anger treatments.

Definitions

The terms anger, irritability, aggression, hostility and violence are commonly used, yet there does not seem to be an absolute definition of any of them. This ambiguity is often referred to when reading the literature. Similarly, when talking to clients and some fellow professionals, it becomes clear that the terms are often clumped together in people's minds.

For the purpose of this manual the following definitions will be used.

Anger can be understood as a subjective emotional state defined by the presence of physiological arousal and cognitions of antagonism (Novaco 1994b). It is a normal emotion having many adaptive features, yet when the frequency, intensity or duration of anger outweigh its adaptive features, it is said to be dysfunctional (Novaco 1992).

Spielberger (1988) divided anger into two types, trait anger (the individual differences of disposition) and state anger (the temporary emotional state arising from frustration or annoyance of the moment). The division was an attempt to separate the personality factors peculiar to individuals from the external factors that could anger any of us.

Irritability has been defined as the tendency to react impulsively, controversially or rudely at the slightest provocation or disagreement (Capara 1986). The term irritability is often used within the Brain Injury literature (Alderman 2003, Kim et al. 1999) as it is a significant neuropsychiatric consequence of acquired brain injury. It can reflect either an internal subjective state or a behaviour arising from this.

Aggression refers to overt behaviour, either physical or verbal, that does or could bring harm to another person, object or system (Eckhardt and Deffenbacher 1995). Barratt (1994) classifies aggression broadly into three categories: (1) premeditated or learned aggression, which varies between social groups and cultures; (2) medically related aggression, which may be secondary to illness, including psychopathology; and (3) impulsive aggression, which is characterised by a 'hair-trigger' temper. This is a helpful categorisation when considering the role of anger in aggression.

Hostility is a personality trait referring to appraisal and cognitive processes through which the individual tends to code others' actions as harmful and unjustified attacks (Eckhardt and Deffenbacher 1995). Hostility reflects a long-standing style of appraisal. It may evoke anger or a cold detachment, or prompt the planning and/or implementation of a vengeful act. This is in contrast to an isolated angry or aggressive response triggered by a specific provocation.

Violence comprises those acts in which there is a deliberate attempt to inflict physical harm; thus accidental harm does not comprise violence (Breakwell 1989).

There is considerable overlap between aggression and violence, the former often being used by psychologists and behavioural biologists, whereas someone with a legal background may use the term violence. Consequently, in the text of this manual the term aggression will be used.

What causes anger?

It is widely assumed that anger occurs as a result of frustration, perceived threat or a belief that a personal injustice has occurred. Common triggers are social or interpersonal in nature. They may be related to a direct external situation, such as being thwarted ('*he made me angry*'), or internal stimuli, such as memories when 'running old tapes'. A person experiencing an image of her friend laughing at her may feel embarrassed (*she's always taking the piss!*) and then incensed; or a sense of injustice, if an expectation is not met (*I have lost my watch and can't find it. I should be able to!)*

The eventual state of anger arousal may also originate as anxiety. Hence if a person is not keeping up with a conversation their initial interpretation (*What's he on about? I can't follow this – I feel stupid!)* will lead to physiological symptoms of anxiety. This arousal may then covert to anger if the cognitions change (*He should speak properly. Why are people always doing this to me?)*. Once aroused, the cognitive functions will be less effective. Consequently the person's attention, abstract reasoning and social inferential ability will deteriorate. This can lead to further anger, as the person is primed to misjudge situations, detect sarcasm and miss humour or is quick to take offence (Hartley 1995).

All of this can be influenced by a person's pre-anger state, i.e. how tired, grumpy, hot, hungry and stressed they are, and also how busy the environment is. Hence, Novaco (1994b) sees anger as an affective stress reaction and it is suggested that this can be magnified if a person has difficulty recognising, managing and/or expressing emotions.

Our clients will have been exposed to unwelcome life experiences, are probably not living in a place of their choice, and are attempting to cope with an impairment and/or physical disability. As such, it is likely that they may feel a loss of autonomy, frustration, injustice and anger. In this case, anger may have had a temporary role in blocking out painful feelings such as loss, grief or a low self-esteem; however, long-term anger obstructs progress.

Organic reasons for anger and irritability

Acquired brain injury, either congenital, or following trauma, or illness, can lead to organic damage to the parts of the brain which are involved in controlling emotional behaviour and tolerance of frustration (frontal lobes and limbic system). This leaves the client with poor control over emotional impulses. (Powell 2004).

Higher anger scores were associated with organic diagnosis, history of aggression and hospital assault data in older adults (Taylor, DuQueno and Novaco, 2004).

There may also be cognitive changes, for example verbal abstraction or inability to appreciate humour (Shammi and Stuss 1999) which may prime the person to misinterpret situations or take offence too readily.

Does anger cause aggression?

As stated, there is considerable overlap between anger, hostility and aggression, yet one does not necessarily lead to the other. An angry person may or may not express their anger, and if they do, it can be in a variety of forms. Some may be aggressive towards other people or objects, but others may be adaptive, for example when using assertion.

The relationship between anger and aggression has been well articulated by Novaco (1994a). Subsequent research in: psychiatric and forensic populations (Hilton and Frankel 2003, McNeil, Eisner and Binder 2003, Novaco, Ramm and Black 2000, O'Neill 1995); incarcerated adolescents (Cornell, Peterson and Richards 1999, Lochman and Lenhart 1993); male offenders with developmental disabilities; (Novaco and Taylor 2004) and those who have suffered acquired brain injury (Medd and Tate 2000) has also shown that anger can be a predictor of aggression.

Likewise, not all aggression is caused by anger (Howells 1989). Some aggression can be seen as instrumental. It is not fuelled by a strong emotional bias but by achieving a desired effect or goal, for example to intimidate or bully another person. This is different from angry, hostile aggression where anger and high levels of affect drive behaviour. This distinction is very relevant in the case of managing problematic anger. A client presenting with instrumental aggression that has a 'pay-off' is unlikely to be motivated to change their behaviour. In contrast, a client who is overwhelmed by their escalating anger and 'hair-trigger' temper may show impulsive aggression, only to regret it later.

A model of anger

The Novaco model of anger was originally described by Novaco (1994a) but was also shown in O'Neill (1995). The model takes a contextual view of anger and places emphasis on environmental factors as well as internal processes.

> The basic conception is that anger is a subjective emotional state, entailing the presence of physiological arousal and cognitions of antagonism, and is a causal determinant of aggression. The 'subjective affect' element of anger is a cognitive labelling of the emotional state as 'angry' or something semantically proximate, such as 'annoyed', 'irritated' or 'provoked'. This cognitive labelling is a highly automatic process, neither deliberate nor necessarily in tandem to the arousal. Associated with this cognitive labelling process is an inclination to act in an antagonistic or confrontational manner towards the source of the provocation. This action impulse is regulated by inhibitory mechanisms (internal and external controls), which may be overridden by disinhibitory influences (such as heightened arousal, aggressive modelling, low probability of punishment, biochemical agents, and contextual cues for aggression). Although provoking events are typically aversive (something the person would choose to avoid), people may engineer their own anger experiences by deliberate exposure to either external or internal stimuli; the arousal of anger may be satisfying as well as being functional.
>
> The relationship of anger to aggression is that it is a significant activator of and has a mutually influenced relationship with aggression, but it is neither necessary nor sufficient for aggression to occur (Novaco 1994a, pages 32–33).

This forms a sound framework that underpins assessment and treatment interventions. The Novaco anger treatment procedure is a cognitive-behavioural treatment originally based on the stress inoculation approach developed by Meichenbaum (1975, 1985), and also drawing on the many works of Beck and Ellis.

An outline of the training procedure follows.

OUTLINE OF THE STRESS INOCULATION TREATMENT FOR ANGER CONTROL

The treatment is a three-stage procedure and, although they are described sequentially, in practice they are interrelated within treatment sessions. It seems necessary also to include a preparatory stage when working with more complex cases (Renwick, Black, Ramm and Novaco 1997; Taylor, Novaco, Gillmer and Robertson 2004) and this will be referred to once again on page 48.

Cognitive preparation

This stage lays down the foundations of any changes that may be made throughout treatment. It includes assessment and interview, and is a time when the therapist and client begin to form a collaborative working relationship. The aim is to reach joint goals of treatment and establish a therapeutic alliance. During this stage, the individual is encouraged to develop an understanding of the components of his or her anger, how it differs from aggression and how the two are related. Training on emotional awareness and self-monitoring may be necessary because this is required before there can be a specific focus on anger.

The positive as well as the negative features of anger are discussed and a cost/benefit analysis carried out. It is pointed out that anger management is not about 'taking away the anger'; indeed, Novaco stresses that many individuals would be afraid of 'being robbed of their anger', feeling that it would also rob them of their ability to stop aversive situations. Instead, the training is meant to empower the individual, allowing him or her to become an expert in understanding and dealing with his or her own anger arousal.

A person's perception of his or her own anger and/or aggression is important, and may in turn relate to his or her motivation to change. If anger is seen to be a benefit rather than a cost, treatment interventions will be resisted. It is worth noting that these costs may not be the same to the individual concerned as they are to his or her family, spouse, fellow clients or the treatment team. If an individual clings to his or her anger, or if it pays dividends, he or she is unlikely to form a collaborative working relationship. Therefore, this stage involves client education and establishes the necessary therapeutic alliance.

Skill acquisition phase

This stage involves teaching cognitive-behavioural coping techniques that can be used when there is a sense of provocation. The individual is trained to see anger as a warning sign of which to take heed, and to decide upon which course of action to take; for example, he or she may ignore the provocation – *'there's no hope of winning'* – and concentrate on reducing arousal levels or use assertion to express effectively a justified annoyance. As these coping skills become more effective, confidence levels increase. The individual has, therefore, a wider choice of response rather than simply resorting to anger and/or aggression. This is an important message to get across because it can promote compliance with this treatment.

In order to provide a structured way of implementing this, the process considers the three components of anger arousal (cognitive, arousal and behavioural) in turn. However, some of the techniques used, such as self-monitoring using cognitive-behavioural diaries or self-instruction, are applicable to each component.

1. The cognitive component

This part of the treatment attempts to change overt behaviour by altering thoughts, interpretations, assumptions and strategies of responding.

Honest self-monitoring is required here, and by using diaries it is possible to gain access to the individual's 'hot cognitions'. This allows both the person concerned and the therapist to become aware of the following:

- The potential triggers on which the individual focuses (one can only get angry about something if one notices it in the first place), such as particular people, their habits, events, comments. Hence biases of attentional focus are identified.
- The individual's appraisal of a situation, including expectation of himself

or herself and others. This will reflect styles of processing and encoding information, memory biases and belief systems.

- Thoughts that may fuel anger (wind-up thoughts). These may be automatic and just happen as if by reflex, or self-statements that a person regularly tells themselves.

The self-monitoring leads to identification of negative or wind-up thoughts. Techniques to interrupt and arrest these wind-up thoughts are learned and, at the same time, arousal reduction is implemented. This allows individuals to then use the techniques of cognitive restructuring in order to challenge or moderate irrational thoughts and unrealistic expectations. Training modifies attentional focus and therefore provides a balance to the interpretation of an incident.

The individual is trained to use self-instruction to direct himself or herself in a controlled way. Self-instruction statements can be used, for example:

(a) when preparing for what may be a provoking situation: *remember, stick to the issues and don't take it personally*
(b) when confronting and handling anger: *don't make more of this than you have to; you don't have to prove yourself*
(c) when reducing levels of arousal: *my muscles are getting tight, time to relax*
(d) after the 'incident'

- if the conflict was unresolved and there's no hope of agreement: *let's agree to disagree, you can't win them all*
- when the conflict was resolved: *I handled that well, that was an improvement.*

Much anger arousal is caused by an individual's personal interpretation of problems, including who is to blame. The style of problem-solving thinking shown determines whether the individual perceives a problem as a catastrophe, or a surmountable task. Some clients may never have acquired problem-solving skills. Others have done so, but their ability to use them will deteriorate at times of high arousal when processing of information is poor. Therefore learning problem-solving routines is part of the treatment.

2. The arousal component

Self-monitoring of bodily changes, such as increased rate of heartbeat, breathing, sweating and muscle tension, is helpful not only in raising awareness of the physical effects of anger but also to provide a measure of the extent of arousal against which any change can be measured.

Progressive relaxation techniques (Jacobson 1938) are recommended as the main form of direct arousal reduction. These are introduced early in the course of training so that the individual has the opportunity to learn and practise the relaxation. The intention is that the individual will learn to appreciate the difference between his or her body being tense and being relaxed.

As the skill is developed, the techniques can be applied at times of arousal and also on a regular basis to keep arousal levels generally low. Imagery is used to allow the individual to relax during a well-known provocation. Gradually the individual becomes able to carry out a shortened version of the techniques that he or she can use to complement the less direct methods of reducing arousal, such as self-instruction, cognitive restructuring or modifying the environment.

3. The behavioural component

Training provides an opportunity for individuals to increase their ability to:

(a) Communicate anger in a way that is effective yet not aggressive. This follows the principles of social skills and assertion training (Liberman, DeRisi and Mueser 1989) and includes the verbal and non-verbal components of behaviour.

(b) Use a systematic problem-solving approach when faced with anger arousal. Initially this process is lengthy but, with training and practice, it becomes quicker and is used automatically.

All three of the components of skill acquisition are important, but clearly some clients may require a greater emphasis on one aspect of training. For example, some clients do not have the necessary assertion skills and have therefore developed a pattern of aggressive behaviour in order to get their point across. Others may have adequate behavioural skills but are quick to perceive a threat or injustice and react accordingly.

Application training

As the training progresses, the range of situations that the individual finds provoking becomes apparent (through self-monitoring and discussion). This phase of the training uses role-play and homework to allow the individual to practise his or her new coping skills. If the situations are presented in a hierarchical order, i.e. the least provoking leading up to the most provoking, the individual should have the opportunity to cope in increasingly difficult situations. This, in turn, encourages increased confidence, reduces the fear of losing control and consequently improves self-esteem.

Summary of key components

- therapeutic engagement
- client education about anger – functional and dysfunctional
- self-monitoring of anger frequency, intensity and triggers
- provocation hierarchy formed from self-monitoring data; this is used when practising coping skills
- arousal reduction techniques of progressive relaxation, breathing techniques and imagery
- cognitive restructuring by altering attentional focus, modifying appraisals, problem-solving thinking and using self-instruction
- behavioural skill development in communication and assertiveness through role-play
- collecting positive evidence of coping
- practising new skills using visualisation and role-play with progressively more anger-provoking scenes.

Does the treatment work?

The stress inoculation approach has been found to be effective with a wide range of populations (for reviews see Novaco 1994b, Tafrate 1995, Edmondson and Conger 1996, Beck and Fernandez 1998, Taylor 2002).

There are, of course, limitations to anger treatments. Ambivalence about therapy and non-attendance is common with out-patients (Siddle, Jones and Awenat 2003). Some clients are very resistant to change (DiGiuseppe et al. 1994) and those who are seriously disturbed are a particular challenge (Howells 1989, Novaco 1997). The history, the meaning of any aggressive behaviours (see page 38), and therefore, motivation to change, have to be acknowledged. The attribution that the person has formed regarding their current state can also interfere with progress. An innocent victim of an accident or assault will also need additional cognitive behavioural therapy to allow them to grieve, acknowledge what has changed, and then learn strategies that ensure they get the best out of themselves. In this case, anger treatment needs to be part of a cohesive programme.

It also has to be acknowledged that some inpatient settings may actually contribute to increased stress and anger levels (Black et al. 1997, Levey and Howells 1991, Taylor 2002). Environmental changes and education for all members of the treatment team may be required before attempting to implement treatment successfully in such a setting.

ADAPTING THE EXISTING TREATMENT TO SUIT CLIENTS WITH COGNITIVE IMPAIRMENT

Establishing the need

Clearly, when working with those individuals who have cognitive impairment, the above treatment intervention has to be simplified. A number of difficulties are immediately apparent, but others were discovered only as the modified version evolved in practice. These are identified below.

- This group may require preliminary work to cope with the identification, discrimination, labelling and then articulation of the feelings of anger. Education on the terms anger and anxiety, and indeed on the normality of emotions in general, will assist the individuals to engage in treatment. For pre-sessional work see page 68.
- Extracting the social meaning of a situation by analysing information from other people and the environment (social cognition) is a challenge for this group. It is dependent upon observation, language skills and information processing capacity. Feedback from others and extra training in observation to highlight the importance of non-verbal behaviours may be necessary.
- The cognitive component of the treatment intervention, in particular, is difficult or impossible for some individuals to comprehend. Identifying 'hot cognitions' or potential anger triggers, and then remembering them, requires both awareness and memory.
- Impaired executive functioning (dysexective syndrome) leading to

increased distractibility, poor monitoring, attentional and memory defects necessitate a modified style when delivering treatment.

- Acquiring the skills of cognitive reappraisal or alternative interpretation of statements requires a great deal of teaching and is dependent on well-developed cognitive communication (Hartley 1995).
- If verbal memory is poor yet the emotional memory strong, the individual may remember the strong affect associated with the anger but not the reappraisal or end result. This affect may be re-triggered by a current event such as seeing 'that person' again; any resulting behavioural response can then appear unreasonable if the situation was previously resolved (LeDoux, 1996).
- The self-monitoring component can seem an insurmountable hurdle to both the therapist and the individual concerned and consequently is often abandoned.
- The progressive relaxation method used is lengthy and exacting. Individuals may not be able to concentrate for, or attend to, the recommended time of practice (up to an hour) each day.
- In order for the principles of Jacobson to be followed precisely, the user must have sufficient comprehension to follow the specific instructions, and also the powers to discriminate between muscle groups.
- It was found that some individuals disliked the tense and relax procedure. Indeed, some were unable to 'let go' after all the muscle tensing and were more comfortable with a stretching movement such as that described by Mitchell (1977, 1987). This point is particularly relevant if the person has a physical disability especially spasticity.
- Some individuals were resistant to participation in any relaxation techniques and refused to associate them with a soaring temper (O'Neill 1997).

Additional influences

So the task was to simplify, yet retain the core components of, the stress inoculation procedure for anger control. This was achieved by looking to the field of learning disability, brain injury and self-management skill training, as well as applying many practical teaching ideas acquired during clinical practice.

A core ingredient of stress inoculation is self-instruction; this fits comfortably with many of the self-management skills taught to those individuals with learning disabilities and brain injury. Coping or cue cards – a prompt to take alternative action – are a practical idea from self-management and anxiety management training. The need to take, and use, the material out of the treatment room is a particular challenge to those with memory problems. Compensatory strategies such as visual reminders, written or spoken scripts, or prompts from trusted others are needed.

Modifications have to be made in the style and speed of delivering treatment, and these are described further later in the text. The search for suitable relaxation and arousal reduction techniques was extensive. It included a review of some well-established methods including – Benson (1985); Mitchell (1987); Schilling and Poppen (1983); all described in Payne (1995, 2000). It also considered a discrete influence that is a result of personal use of yoga techniques.

A literature search revealed that behavioural relaxation training (BRT) has been shown to be effective with those with a mental handicap (Williams 1990). This method was found to be more easily understood by clients than was abbreviated progressive relaxation training (APR) Lindsay, Overend, Allan and Williams (1998); see Appendix 1. In BRT the person, who is seated in a comfortable chair rather than lying down, observes and imitates a series of easily demonstrated postures or observable states of relaxation. This procedure acknowledges the reluctance of some individuals to lie down during a group session. It also does not allow the relaxation to be dismissed by the user as a passive activity that has little relevance in those heated moments.

As the relaxation and arousal reduction methods are introduced in the manual, the reader will, therefore, detect influences from many sources. Although methods are suggested, they are by no means prescriptive. Many therapists have a great deal of experience in using relaxation training with their clients and, as such, have determined the methods most suitable.

The evolution of OTSAR

The component of '**O**n **T**he **S**pot **A**rousal **R**eduction' (see Appendix 1, page 165) evolved initially as a way of reducing levels of arousal for clients who were not keen to carry out traditional relaxation. It later proved to meet a need for a practised technique that could be used easily at times of anger arousal. It is the result of experience and user feedback.

For some individuals who are resistant to the term relaxation, this form of arousal reduction is a creative way of learning a relaxation response. So OTSAR (O'Neill 1997) can be used as an alternative to, or to complement, full relaxation. Luckily the complete title of the technique does not have to be used and the acronym OTSAR revealed itself as a great source of amusement for many clients and fellow occupational therapists or OTs. OTSAR has the potential to be customised and many individuals have recordings of their personalised scripts (own voice or that of the therapist) to use when they monitor increasing anger arousal.

Summary

This modified version of the stress inoculation procedure for anger control has been used with individuals who have varying degrees of cognitive impairment. Experience has shown that many such individuals are able to recognise increasing levels of anger arousal and can be taught a sequence of events to follow in response to that arousal. This may include a personal cue such as 'you're getting near your Ne-Nar zone', or visualisation of the traffic lights and self-instruction – 'I'm in the orange, better get back to the green'.

The sequence then continues with self-instruction to carry out OTSAR, either to provide a lasting solution, i.e. cooling down and using distraction, or to inhibit the arousal until the individual can problem solve or seek external help. Once again situations are presented in a hierarchical order to allow the individual to cope in increasingly difficult situations. This process is a 'scaling down' of the cognitive-behavioural model, with the greater emphasis being placed on the behavioural coping skills, whilst still acknowledging the role of the cognitions.

DELIVERING ANGER TREATMENT

THERAPISTS

Experience

Whether group or individual treatment is delivered, therapists will need to learn the specific cognitive-behavioural techniques of stress inoculation. It is expected that they will have developed knowledge and experience of cognitive-behavioural techniques, such as anxiety management, and will have undertaken wider reading on the subject of anger and its management.

If treatment is to be delivered in groups, it is necessary to have a regular therapist and co-therapist. Certainly one, and ideally both, should have undertaken additional training on anger management. However, if this has not been possible, any experience gained in running skill-building groups, such as social skills training, assertion or problem-solving is relevant because these are all components of managing anger (see Components of Managing Anger diagram on page 26). Therapists will also need to have a regular supervision session in which to discuss cases, the therapeutic relationship, and receive objective input on any problematic situations.

Exercise for the therapist to complete

What is different about working with angry people?

As was said earlier (page 10), the emotion anger has a great deal in common with the emotion anxiety. There are biological similarities, but the cognitive content is very different, as are the possible behavioural responses. Yet do we have different thoughts and feelings about working with angry clients?

Write down what is different about working with angry or anxious people then read on before we revisit this exercise.

Components of managing anger

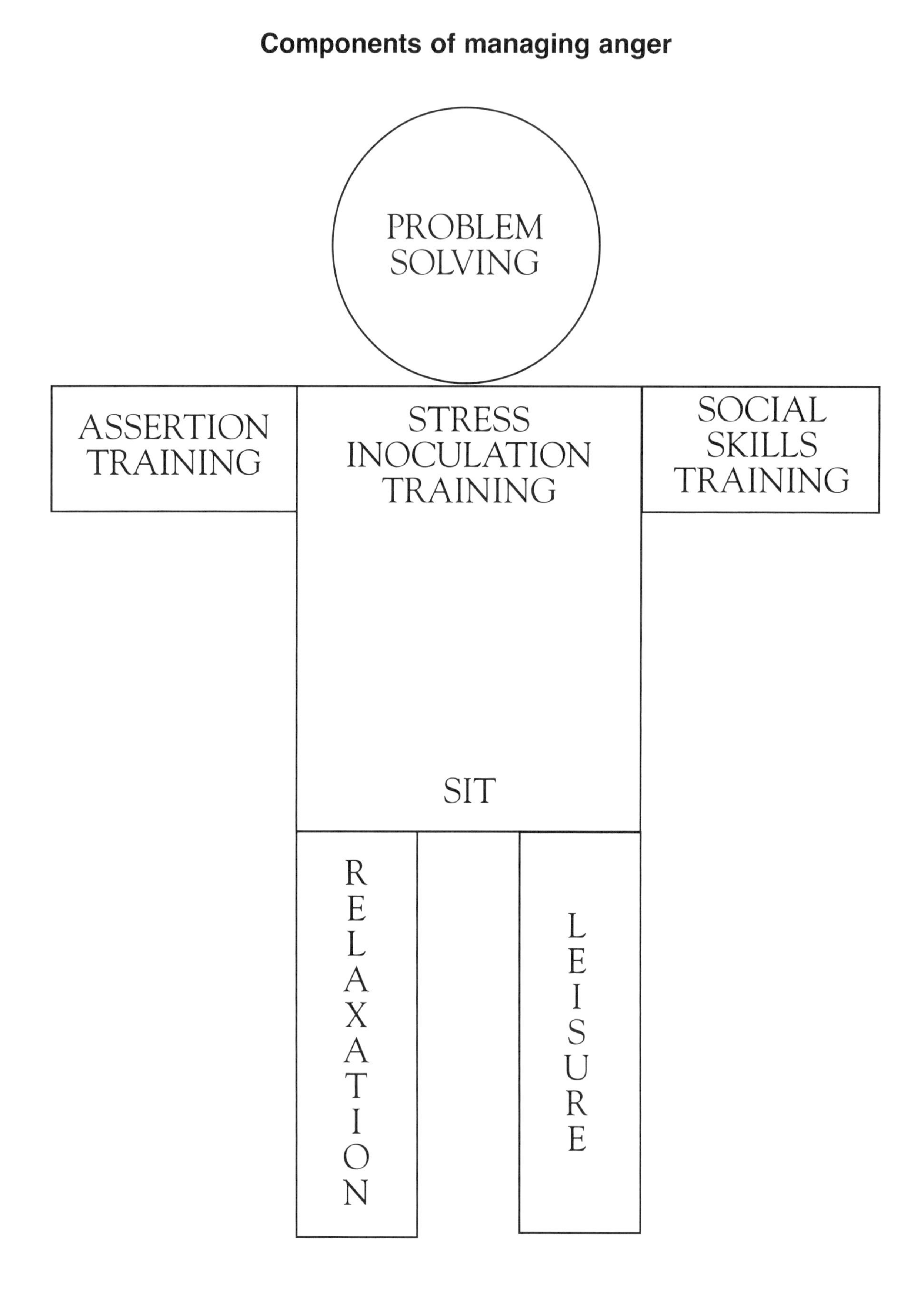

Self-awareness

It is advisable for therapists to spend time considering their understanding of anger both in themselves and others. Any therapist delivering anger treatments will be exposed to a great deal of anger expressed both orally and in written form in diaries. Anger arousal can be infectious. Therefore, when working in close proximity to clients who are communicating their levels of anger, it is wise to remember that this process can evoke strong feelings within those who are listening. The therapist is no exception to this and will, like everyone else, have his or her own anger triggers. If the therapist either identifies with, or is too distressed by, the anger reported by others, his or her own personal feelings could potentially affect the delivery of treatment and the therapeutic relationship.

The therapist's own beliefs and assumptions about both the client's behaviour and their own performance as a therapist are influential. We all have our own 'shoulds, oughts and musts' and our 'beliefs about challenging behaviours are likely to be significant factors in understanding the manner in which we respond to challenging behaviour' (Morgan and Hastings 1998). Likewise, personal standards such as – *I should not dislike a patient*, and *I must help all clients*, whilst admirable, are demanding, unrealistic and may affect how we respond.

Now revisit the earlier exercise, here are some examples of thoughts that have come from staff training sessions:

<table>
<tr><th>When working with a client who has
Anxiety</th><th>When working with a client who has
Anger + Aggression</th></tr>
<tr><td>• I feel more confident and equipped to cope
• Feel more sympathetic
• Anxiety is more acceptable
• Women seem to disclose it more readily than men do
• They seem like a victim?
• It's easier to have empathy for clients
• I give a gentle approach
• Has a diagnosis, so it is a real condition</td><td>• What are the risk factors ?
• It can be less predictable
• I feel nervous
• Client may be less likely to admit to their problem, so harder to help
• Client may present as a bully
• Anger has more impact on others
• I have to try harder to listen
• Not so sure what I'm dealing with</td></tr>
<tr><td colspan="2">Do you relate to these thoughts?</td></tr>
</table>

So what is different about working with angry people? Obviously the worst case scenarios could be very different. Yet the two emotions are often related, for example:

A client is finding an everyday task difficult. He feels instant physiological arousal and anxious thoughts, 'Oh, I can't do this. I feel a real prat!' His cognitions then change to angry thoughts 'This is rubbish. Why the Hell did they give it to me to do? They do it on purpose!' Then his physiological arousal is reinterpreted and experienced as anger. This is a common pattern of anger. Clients who struggle to come to terms with their cognitive or physical impairments may cope by externally dumping the anger on someone else, in order to save face or bolster their low self-esteem.

It short, it may be easier, or more natural, to feel empathy for an anxious person rather than someone who feels angry/aggressive.

Anger may evoke more judgement than anxiety does

Therefore the therapist needs to ask himself or herself the following questions:

- What do I mean by anger? Consider semantics and labelling.
- Am I clear about the difference between anger and aggression?
- Have I thought about my own views on anger and its expression? These will depend on, experience, upbringing, culture and religion. Do I respect differences in the views of others?
- Is anger ever justified, and if so does that alter treatment?
- Is anger always damaging or is it useful?
- Am I aware of my own anger triggers?
- What is my attitude towards a client who has shown a lot of anger and/or aggression towards others? Do I remember to distinguish between the person and their behaviours?
- Am I judgemental or can I retain a sense of enquiry in order to try to understand (though not necessarily approve) of others' feelings and behaviours? Will any disgust of a client's previous behaviour affect the therapeutic relationship? Can I respect that their background may have necessitated anger and aggression?
- Am I prepared to listen to reports of anger – some will be about other staff members – and can I remain impartial?
- Do I have sufficient resilience and support to cope with such exposure?

THE THERAPEUTIC RELATIONSHIP

Establishing a common goal

If the treatment is to be effective, there is a need for both the therapist and the client to have a common goal of treatment. This may be quickly established if anger is a problem to the client because it causes them distress or if the perceived or actual costs of the anger weigh heavily.

Yet even if a client accepts that anger is a problem to them, their initial plan may not be to change their own anger, but instead to try to change those people with whom they are angry, i.e. the others! A common expression is: *Yes I do get angry and it's a problem, but they cause it so they must change, not me!*

Whilst we have to acknowledge that anger can be a natural warning sign that something is unfair or a violation, it can also be a sign that a person's appraisal of a situation is biased or irrational. To then place the blame on others is a common external attribution. This might be comfortable to live with but it does not encourage the client to take any responsibility for their emotion and behaviour. Such an attribution may be voiced frequently in the early stages of treatment and it highlights both the client's fear of change and their lack of understanding about the management of problematic anger. They may assume that they will be expected never to feel angry and to extinguish all expression of anger, thus leaving them to be seen as a 'pushover', rather than learning to evaluate the anger more carefully and, if it is justified, to assert their views.

Hence, there needs to be a collaborative process of discovery, which contributes to forming the therapeutic alliance. This process of discovery needs to include some acknowledgement of cognitive skill deficits that may prime the person for anger. Memory problems are a good example. Individuals who have a poor memory may be inclined to feel angry either with themselves or with others whom they believe have taken advantage of them. This assumption can then hinder the setting of a common goal until the deficit plus the use of necessary memory strategies are validated.

The therapeutic alliance

One of the assumptions associated with cognitive behaviour therapy is that clients can engage in a collaborative relationship within the first few sessions. When working with an angry client this is not easily fulfilled. It may take much longer than it would with a client being treated for other emotional problems, and happen only after considerable effort on behalf of the therapist. Yet it is necessary to achieve this if any thorough work is to be done.

DiGiuseppe (1995) talks about the necessity of establishing a therapeutic alliance between client and therapist. This alliance is more than the therapeutic relationship that is referred to in psychotherapy, and includes an agreement between therapist and client on the goals and tasks of therapy. This agreement can sometimes be difficult to reach with an angry client who may hold certain beliefs, about himself or others, that make a need to change seem unnecessary. For example:

- *I must express my anger in order to get rid of it.* This belief that cathartic release is effective as a way of reducing arousal is not supported by research (Tavris 1989). In fact 'talking it out' or directing it at something or somebody, often prolongs or increases the arousal, and at worst, rehearses the anger, unless followed by some reappraisal of the cause of the anger.
- *This is how I am, I'll never change!* This belief reflects deep hopelessness. Upbringing, life events or disability all fuel such a belief.
- *If you don't show your anger you're weak and a pushover!* This belief is commonly held if the client was raised in an environment where adults showed anger in order to discipline, so no shouting meant no power.

Such beliefs may hinder a client's motivation to change and the forming of a therapeutic alliance (Prochaska and DiClemente 1982). These beliefs will have to be discovered and then gently challenged in a way that will not cause the client threat or alienation. It will be necessary to validate any loss, pain or grief whilst maintaining a sense of hope that things can change. The therapist will need to decide if this should be in a group setting or, more likely, individually. The former can give group support whilst what are often commonly held beliefs about anger are dispelled; the latter offers an opportunity for in-depth understanding at a pace ideal for the client. At all times, the therapist has to show empathy with the client, and earn the privilege of hearing their disclosures without blame or judgement.

LISTENING TO A PERSON REPORTING THEIR ANGER

Within therapy sessions the therapist will need to facilitate individuals to recount their anger experiences. Yet as a person does this it is likely that they may experience anger arousal once again. The therapist may feel on the receiving end of the anger, particularly if criticism is directed at team members. Remember that any 'hot cognitions' reported in a session were, at the time of anger arousal, real to the person concerned. Many of these cognitions may be distorted, hence the person's need for anger management training. A therapist must not adopt a defensive response when listening, as this will inhibit the client's reporting and recording; instead use an active listening style.

Hints:

- Listen to the person's point of view and try to put yourself in their place. Do not go into problem solving mode just yet.
- Do not become immediately defensive, as from then on you won't hear properly. Keep your own level of arousal down and arrest the cognitions by SIT such as: *they are angry at the situation, not me.*
- Use short responses and then do allow them time to process any information before responding.
- When in an angry **STATE,** the person really believes that they are in the right; that is therefore not the best time to challenge.
- However illogical it may sound, this is what the person was thinking at the time.
- Acknowledge that you can accept that that is what they felt (it doesn't mean you have to agree with it!).
- Encourage reporting of facts rather than venting of anger.
- Redirect the feelings about people towards future solutions.

- Try to understand what needs they are trying to meet.
- Encourage the person to reduce their level of arousal before confronting any problems.

Don't automatically give advice or instruction:

- *Now calm down!*
- *Take a deep breath.*
- *You've got this wrong.*
- *I've met lots of people with this sort of problem and what you need to do is . . . .*
- *Now don't be silly!*
- *We told you this would happen!*

Or pretend to understand as this can sound condescending:

- *I know how you feel!*
- *Yes, this is something I often hear.*

Instead have a warm tone, show empathy, use their name, and talk clearly and calmly. Discourage rambling and try statements such as:

- *Take your time and tell me exactly what happened.*
- *So it all started when…*
- *Take one step at a time.*
- *I'm going to bring you back to … we're getting off track*
- *Well, it does sound as if you could have a point there.*
- *I can see that you are upset/angry* (use their word).
- *So you felt really………*(reflect)
- *Oh Fred as you tell me all of that I realise I'm getting tense too, so let's just get calm …………..*
- *It's not really me you are angry with, is it?*
- *I can tell you've had a bad time and now this must seem like the last straw for you.*

If possible, encourage the person to:

- Sit down. However, they may not want to sit down, they may see it as 'backing down' or 'giving in', or they may be too aroused to settle.
- Use any breathing techniques that you know they have learned previously, e.g. diaphragmatic breathing.

- Breathe out or sigh, then take two deep breaths – *breathe away the anger.*

At the end of the communication stand up slowly and do not make any hasty movements for they could be perceived as threatening.

DE-ESCALATION TECHNIQUES

These skills are needed in order to defuse a situation in a group setting or with a highly charged individual (Paterson, Leadbetter and McComish 1997, McDonnell 1999). When faced with an angry person and if you can sense the warning signs:

- Know where the exit is – look discreetly.
- Take all threats seriously.
- Bring your voice level up slightly and use the person's name.
- Stay out of the person's space.
- Do not make sudden moves. It can appear threatening and they may be frightened as well as angry.
- If you want to move don't just step back, instead make a side turn.
- Keep an open posture.
- Breathe slowly and be aware of your own level physiological arousal.
- Think calmly.
- Use only fleeting eye contact, as direct eye contact can be construed as threatening or baiting.
- Encourage the person to distance themselves from the provoking cues.
- Move from a public setting to a quieter one (if you feel safe) – *let's go to the …….. and discuss it.*
- Stay calm – don't argue back and keep an even tone of voice.
- Allow the other person to save face whenever possible.
- Set limits and reflect how you feel, e.g. *Let's take a few minutes to cool down, and then we will try to solve it. I am willing to listen but when you shout it feels scary.* Give limited options.
- Even an apology can be misinterpreted at this state of arousal; in fact an urgent repeated apology can seem like a provocation!

- 'When the anger is up, the judgement is down', so this is not the best time for reasoning or expecting the person to problem-solve.

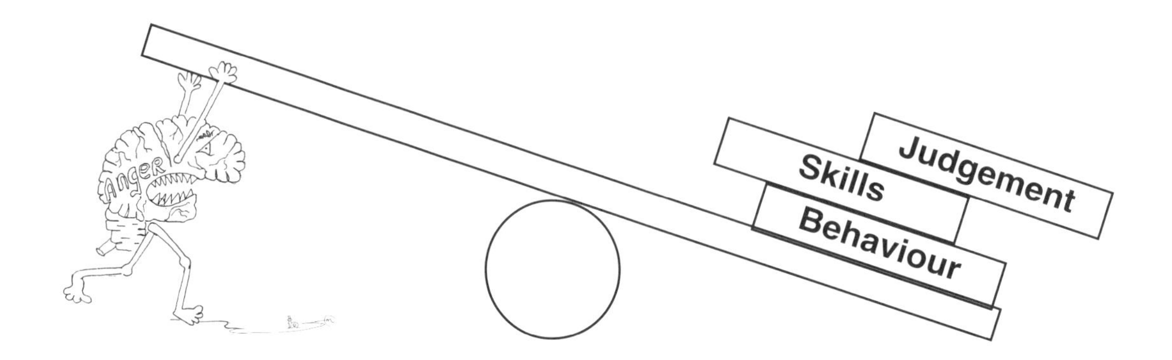

Remember:
- An angry person is quick to perceive threat, harm or injustice. Their attentional focus is primed to look for it!
- Cognitive processing is at its worst at times of arousal.
- It is natural to 'mood match' but we can't match a person's anger.
- Yet if we are too calm this could be interpreted as not listening or caring, in which case they may try even harder to get the message across, and therefore shout even louder!

Aim to be controlled but concerned ↓ reflected by tone of voice, gestures and facial expression

If possible don't avoid the angry person after the episode is over.

CHECKLIST FOR SUITABILITY

Before delivering managing anger sessions, therapists will need skill to:

- maintain the focus of the group/session
- be flexible during sessions to ensure a balance between covering planned session material and capitalising on useful learning situations that arise during the feedback
- develop a knack of eliciting the key points in feedback
- be a facilitator and a teacher, using active listening skills
- interpret the comments of the group members without altering their meaning
- observe group dynamics and reactions as anger-evoking situations are discussed or re-enacted
- redirect the feeling of blame about others towards finding solutions
- organise role-play, using video equipment if it is available
- be mindful of the importance of the therapeutic relationship, particularly if working on an individual basis
- feel comfortable when listening to reports of anger
- be familiar with de-escalation techniques
- be resourceful, unshockable and retain a sense of enquiry rather than judgement.

It is also important to receive regular supervision sessions.

WHICH INDIVIDUALS MIGHT BE SUITABLE FOR ANGER TREATMENTS?

There is not a straightforward answer to this question. As already mentioned anger treatments have been delivered to a wide range of clients. Novaco, Ramm and Black (2000) differentiated between several levels of psychological interventions for anger problems. Clearly clients' needs and level of function predict accessibility to the treatment and the method of delivery. Taylor, Novaco, Gillmer and Robertson (2004) and Whitaker (2001) refer to the range of behavioural and cognitive components of treatment used with the developmental disability population. This reflects that treatment can be delivered at different levels. Therefore, this section can not be absolutely prescriptive, although there are necessary considerations to take into account during assessment.

Initial referral for anger treatment will invariably come from the treatment team. Before it is decided if the referral is appropriate it is important to seek any existing psychological (preferably neuropsychological) and speech and language assessments, and to consult the relevant professionals. The following points need to be considered in order to assess if the person will be able to cope with the treatment and how it would need to be delivered. Assessment methods and tools are described on page 59.

History of behaviour

Information on incidents of aggression and outbursts of anger (obtainable from case notes or incident reports) help to establish what type of aggression the client displays. As stated earlier (see page 11), it is important to distinguish between angry and instrumental aggression, as the latter will not respond to anger treatment. Intimidation and bullying may have become a habit, either because it was learned in early life or is a defensive reaction. Hence, it will be important to attempt to understand the meaning of the behaviour; is it maintained purely because it pays off? Did the client ever experience the reinforcement of using adaptive skills? What are the social norms within their family? Is the behaviour an effective form of communication? Clients with expressive language impairment have been shown to have less behavioural control (Alderman, Knight and Henman 2002).

A functional analysis of the behaviour (McDonnell, Reeves, Johnson and Lane 1998) is required to establish if self-management strategies have a role. For example, the style and speed of delivering information to clients can trigger challenging behaviour (Kevan 2003). Swearing, which can be a form of automatic speech, can become excessive and a common clinical presentation in some neurological disorders (Van Lancker and Cummings 1999); this behaviour is not anger driven and so would not respond to anger management. At other times swearing may be anger driven, but the client may lack the ability to use other alternative language. Therefore it is appropriate to target this behaviour using both speech and language and psychological interventions.

> It is important to remember that there are medically related reasons for aggression. Uncommonly outbursts of explosive aggression can arise with little or no trigger, and it is important that this is properly evaluated as in some instances it will lead to a diagnosis of episodic dyscontrol syndrome and will need drug treatment (Eames and Wood 2003, Golden et al. 1996).

There may have been an obvious onset of the problematic moods and behaviours if the person has experienced psychological trauma, physical disability, pain or a brain injury (Denmark and Gemeinhardt 2002).

Insight and awareness

Some insight into the costs of the anger and resulting behaviours is a necessary requirement. A persistent lack of awareness regarding social behaviours and relationships will hamper the rehabilitation process. Fleming, Strong and

Ashton (1996) note the distinction between organic and psychological disorders of self-awareness. They point out that intellectual awareness is only the first step towards full awareness and they cite Crosson and colleagues' pyramid model of intellectual, emerging and lastly anticipatory awareness. It is important to assess which stage a person is at. Any deficits, or differences, can only be managed if they are acknowledged and compensatory strategies used. When a person has deficits and is not aware of them, then these deficits may prime the person for a sense of justified anger. For example, poor memory or slow processing of information may lead to frustration and anger. Although a greater awareness can be painful and associated with depression, this is a necessary stage to reach, before adopting self-management strategies, and then moving forward.

Sensory impairments

If clients have sensory impairments it is important that these are acknowledged. Many clients have obvious visual, hearing, perceptual or spatial distortions whereas others may have more subtle tactile sensitivity or depth perception problems. It is important that any of these are assessed and acknowledged, because they may well be contributing to their anger arousal.

Motivation

A model for understanding the stages of change in the therapeutic process (Prochaska and DiClemente 1982) shows that clients need to be contemplating change before they can decide to behave differently. If a client perceives their anger as a cost, it is likely that they will be at least partly motivated to learn alternative ways of coping. This may be apparent to the treatment team before assessment or it may become clear during the semi-structured interview. If the client shows a glimmer of motivation, further work, such as a cost/benefits exercise and peer group encouragement (MI techniques see page 63), may enlighten the client on their choice of responses. Novaco (1997) writes that participants must be helped to see that learning anger control skills will help make them more powerful, rather than less powerful. It also has to be acknowledged that the treatment environment may contribute to a client's motivation to change or not, and this is discussed further in the section 'The treatment setting'.

Loss of motivation or drive can have an organic origin, for example, problems with executive functioning such as poor initiation, inability to monitor performance and difficulty using feedback from the environment to regulate behaviour effectively (Alderman and Ward 1991).

Cognitive abilities

Intellectual function

There are no absolute guidelines to cover the level of intellectual function necessary to benefit from the treatment. Black (1990) is one of a number of authors who have noted evidence of functional ability rather than relying purely on IQ. Black, Cullen and Novaco (1997) assert that people with mild learning disabilities can benefit from cognitive behaviour treatments. A more recent study (Taylor, Novaco, Gillmer and Thorne 2002) included patients with a full-scale IQ of between 55 and 80.

Feindler and Ecton (1986) also state that people with borderline or mild learning disability might benefit from anger control treatment, but consider that the development of the language skills is a far more important factor than IQ.

Information processing and memory

Clients with attention or concentration deficits and/or slow speed of processing can benefit from the treatment if the style and speed of delivery are adjusted. Likewise, poor memory need not exclude a client from treatment, indeed it is expected that many clients who have cognitive impairment may have some memory problems and strategies to compensate for this will be described in the session plans.

Language and comprehension

It appears that without the facility of receptive and expressive language, the individuals will not be able to either comprehend others' conversation, or provide themselves with self-guiding statements or self-instruction (Feindler and Ecton 1986). The role of internal speech in developing self-regulation skills that control behaviour is described clearly by Goldstein and Keller (1987). They refer to what happens during the course of a child's normal development when, between the ages of 4.5 and 5.5 years, the child's self-verbalisation shifts from overt to covert (internal) speech. Research showing the relationship between impulsivity and poor verbal control of overt behaviour is cited. Hence, self-instruction has been used to train youngsters to provide themselves with internally generated verbal commands.

Verbally orientated approaches have been shown to help people with learning disabilities (Williams and Jones, 1997) and impaired language skills (Black 1990). Self-instruction strategies have also been used with neurologically impaired adults (O'Callaghan and Couvadelli 1998).

However, many clients in this group have multiple cognitive impairments. Language deficits may be compounded by information processing difficulties and poor memory. Speech and language assessment may reveal a number of difficulties such as:- abstracting the intended meaning, appreciating humour, or a mismatch between receptive and expressive communication (Kevan 2003). If this is the case, the client will have particular problems with social interaction and may require complementary speech and language therapy.

Gilmour (1998) showed that clients require assistance to develop their communication system and express their emotions in appropriate ways.

Executive function

A large variety of cognitive abilities and behavioural symptoms are associated with executive impairment. These include planning, organisation, memory, inhibition, concentration, sustained and divided attention, resistance to interference, self-monitoring, sequencing, impulsivity, perseveration, utilisation of feedback, self-control, cognitive flexibility, problem solving, abstract thinking, ability to deal with novelty, initiation and motivation. Although such impairments have traditionally been linked with traumatic brain injury (TBI), they have also been noted in people with schizophrenia, multiple sclerosis, vascular dementia, Huntington's disease and learning disabilities (Fogel, 1994; Ponsford, Sloan and Snow, 1995). Consequently clients suggested for anger treatment may well have some executive impairment. This will be mentioned further under assessment.

Emotional recognition

Recognition and labelling of emotions in oneself and others is central to the treatment process (Black, Cullen and Novaco 1997). To ensure that the client is able to identify emotions and show some ability to differentiate between thoughts, body feelings and resulting behaviours, preparatory sessions using photos and video may be needed. This is described further as pre-sessional work on page 68. This may be assessed further by using the Awareness of Social Inference Test (TASIT–McDonald, Flanagan and Rollins 2002) or the Facial Expression of Emotion Stimulus Test (FEEST – Young, Perret, Calder, Sprengelmeyer and Eckman 2002).

Ability to self-monitor changes in physiological arousal

Learning to self-monitor and grade the levels of anger is a necessary part of anger management and leads to written, pictorial or colour-coded records. However, before this recording can take place the client needs to be able to register the change in their levels of arousal. If clients have difficulty with this, a simple biofeedback machine can raise their awareness by giving audio or visual feedback. There are a variety of neuro/biofeedback machines available from Relax-UK Ltd.

Note: see also session 2

There are numerous reasons why self-monitoring causes difficulty and these need to be remembered when assessing.

- Recognising the emotion – both physiological arousal and distinguishing it from pain or physical discomfort; and cognitive changes
- No gradual warning signs, instead a sudden surge of emotion: 0 → 100%
- The recording process may re-kindle anger or trigger more emotion, guilt, blame, or fear of disclosure
- The writing may evoke inadequacy and frustration if literacy skills are poor
- Memory – remembering to do it
- Reluctance to change, owning the feeling and behaviour and committing it to paper
- Lack of support from peers, relatives may lead to tactless comments or even ridicule
- Hopelessness – *I can't change so why bother*

CHECKLIST FOR SUITABILITY

Inclusion

- Any aggression shown to objects, others or self is fuelled by anger.
- Is distressed by the anger or by the costs of it, such as resulting restrictions, loss of broken belongings, consequences in relationships.
- Is consenting to treatment. Check they have capacity to consent, and if not, discuss with family, the team and weigh up the alternatives in the client's best interest.
- Psychological and speech and language assessments have been referred to.
- Shows some motivation to engage in treatment, i.e. wants to 'be in charge' of the anger.

  Ability to recognise own anger and self-monitor levels of arousal.
- Often impatient, frustrated and upset by environmental triggers.
- Some degree of literacy is ideal, but not essential.
- May have poor assertion skills.
- May have low self-esteem (see Rosenberg (1965) for measures of self-esteem).

Exclusion

- Shows well-planned, instrumental, rather than angry, aggression.
- Feels his or her anger/aggression pays off and does not want to change.
- Shows active psychosis (such as to interfere with treatment).
- Regular use of drugs/alcohol/solvents.
- Very severe memory problems, unable to retain information, learn from repetition, or written /pictorial hand-outs.
- Comprehension is extremely limited in all modalities.
- Language functioning does not permit use of self-instruction.
- Exclude medical reasons for aggression (Eames and Wood 2003).

GROUP OR INDIVIDUAL TREATMENT?

The cognitive-behavioural techniques of anger management are now used with an increasing range of clients. There are reports of the treatment being delivered both in groups (between three and eight members) and on an individual basis (see examples of studies on page 49). Yet how does the therapist decide which is the most suitable for the client when clearly both have advantages.

Group treatment:

- It is a cost-effective method of delivery.
- The group also helps members appreciate the normality of anger as they listen to the perspective of others. Members may find it reassuring to hear that others also experience problematic anger, and that they too are struggling to manage it in an effective way.
- It is ideal for some of the techniques, such as role-play and assertion training.
- Peers are able to give realistic feedback and reinforcement. This is particularly so if the therapist is working with clients of a different age group or culture from his/her own and is consequently viewed with less credibility.
- A group may seem less threatening, or demand less effort, compared to more intense individual work.
- Given time, group support can develop and, if it does, this can also be a powerful motivating factor even outside the group.
- The group can give support whilst commonly held beliefs about anger are discussed and re-evaluated.

Individual treatment

- The speed and style of delivery of information can be 'tailor-made' to focus on the client's needs, for example writing down the key points of the dialogue as it is spoken, using different coloured pens for both the client and the therapist. This maximises the opportunity for the client to attend, process and remember the material being covered. An added bonus is the written record of any agreed plans. For some such clients the pace of a group may evoke anxiety, frustration, feelings of inadequacy and even disruptive behaviours.

- Some clients have difficulty processing more than one stimulus at any one time and therefore cannot focus their attention if they are in a noisy or busy group setting. Experience has shown that if this is the case, the environmental setting for the delivery of treatment is of paramount importance, and therefore it may be more productive to work individually. (Good work has been wasted because it was delivered in a distracting setting and consequently not attended to, the client having no recollection of it later on.)
- A trusting therapeutic relationship is the key to clients engaging in treatment, so it is important to set a gentle, non-threatening treatment environment where the therapist can earn the clients' trust. In some cases this may be achieved only on an individual basis, either initially, or for the course of treatment.
- Many clients have poor self-esteem; individual sessions can make them feel 'special'. However, the therapist needs to safeguard against dependency.
- Despite agreed group guidelines about confidentiality clients might not disclose details of their own anger patterns as readily in a group. Many clients can be mistrustful both of other clients and of staff members in the group, particularly if the treatment setting is a secure environment. Possible distrust must be taken into account when asking clients to disclose details of their own anger, which for many people leads to a feeling of betrayal and vulnerability when defences are down. If there is an audience at the time of the disclosure, the person may perceive threat, fear or deny the existence of feelings.
- Members may be concerned about being in a mixed gender group.
- The cognitive aspects of anger are very personal and clients may feel that they are not suitable to be unearthed in a group. When clients are living together in the same hospital or community setting, the focus of their anger may be another client in the group. If they report this anger

in the group they may fear retaliation outside the session. Conversely, some clients could attempt to use the group as a public reporting place where they can shame or antagonise other members.
- If more in-depth cognitive restructuring work is necessary, the therapist may choose to do this on an individual basis, but in addition to the group sessions.

If a group is not appropriate or even available, the treatment can be delivered on an individual basis. However, as the skill-building component is covered behavioural experiments or assignments will be needed to enable the client to practise techniques, *in vivo*, outside the treatment room.

DURATION OF TREATMENT

Novaco's treatment procedure (updated 1993–4) was originally devised for outpatients and consisted of 12 90-minute sessions. As the procedure has been used with different populations, the duration of treatment has been adjusted. It is clear that for many clients 12 sessions are not enough. It is also clear that sessions lasting for 90 minutes are too long for many clients. So is it a matter of delivering the original 18 hours of treatment in shorter, perhaps more frequent, bursts? There may be some sense in this, but clearly it is not simply that prescriptive.

For some, 30-minute sessions twice a week will be most suitable. Kellner and Tutin (1995) found that this style of delivery catered for the clients' limited attention span and allowed for frequent repetition and positive reinforcement as skills were acquired. However, if longer sessions can be tolerated they are preferable. There is then adequate time for feedback, and opportunity to cover new material and practise arousal reduction techniques at each session.

A review of the studies published reveals courses of treatment lasting from 6 to 50 sessions (see page 49 for examples). Despite this diversity, the work of Black (1990), Black and Novaco (1993), Taylor et al. (2004), as well as personal experience, shows that when working with the cognitively impaired, the speed of delivery has to be adjusted compared to the original work.

There may be a need to include pre-sessional work that increases the clients' emotional awareness. Some ideas for this are given on page 68. This work primes clients for the main treatment, when they will need to be able to notice, recognise and then self-monitor their anger. An added bonus of this pre-sessional work is that the group members have the opportunity to work together, and hopefully this lays the foundations for self-disclosure, and trust in other members.

Examples of studies, showing the number of treatment sessions:

Number of sessions (Total number of hours)	Length of sessions	Group or individual	Study	Subjects
6 – (6)	1 hr	Individual	Medd and Tate (2000)	28 brain-injured living in the community
12 – (15)	1 – 1.5 hrs	2 individual cases	Uomoto and Brockway (1992)	Brain-injured living in the community
12 – (18)	1.5 hrs	Group	Wilcox and Dowrick (1992)	Adolescents in residential treatment
15 – (37)	2.5hrs with a break	Group	McMurran et al. (2001)	Personality disordered offenders in a medium secure unit
16 – (32)	2 hrs with a break	Group	Rose et al. (2000)	Developmental disabilities in residential treatment
18–(27)	1.5 hrs	Group	Gilmour (1998)	Learning Disabilities community
6 preparatory phase and 12 treatment phase – (18)	1 hr	Individual × 2 per week	Taylor, Novaco, Gillmer and Robertson (2004)	Offenders with developmental disabilities
5 preparatory and 20 treatment phase – (37)	1.5 hrs	Group	Renwick et al. (1997)	Forensic hospital patients
28–(20)	40 mins	Individual	Black and Novaco (1993)	Developmentally handicapped man – hospital
40–(20)	30 mins	Group × 2 per week	Kellner and Tutin (1995)	Developmentally and emotionally disabled high school students
50–(50)	1 hr	Small group × 2 per week	Black (1990)	Mentally handicapped adults

Further studies are reviewed in Denmark and Gemeinhardt (2002) Novaco (1994b, 1997), Taylor (2002), Taylor et al. (2002), Whitaker (2001)

Hence, it is likely that anger management work may take up to four times longer with those clients who have cognitive impairment. An individual's rate of progress will depend on many participant variables, including:

- general cognitive functioning
- motivation
- receptive and expressive communication skills

This will determine the speed of delivery, the amount of repetition needed and the necessary environment for delivery.

Group sessions present another unpredictable variable, i.e. how well the group gels. If a sound, trusting environment develops, the amount of interaction and support generated within the group will increase. In this case to 'hurry through' the stages of treatment may throw away learning opportunities. This is not to say that the therapist should regard the duration of treatment as open-ended. Regular reviews of progress are essential, but a therapist anxious to keep to a tight timescale risks unnecessary pressure on the members, and is left with the haunting question 'have the clients absorbed the session material?'

REMEMBER, SLOW BUT SURE!

Other skill-building sessions may complement the work done in anger management. These are: relaxation, problem-solving, social skills and assertion training (see the diagram on page 26). Often clients are also involved in some of these anyway, but if not, a course of sessions could be offered as a change, or indeed respite, from a long course on managing anger!

Follow-up

Experience has shown that regular follow-up sessions (say monthly) help to reinforce the knowledge and the newly acquired skills. Some individuals seem to need a regular 'top-up' as a maintenance dose of treatment. There is further information on 'bringing the techniques out of the treatment room' and maintaining skills after the course of treatment on page 150.

THE TREATMENT SETTING

Anger must be viewed contextually (Novaco 1993), therefore the effect of the environment in which the client lives must never be underestimated. It will provide its own set of dynamics that may, in turn, be evident within the treatment setting. The therapist needs to remember the implications of this when treating clients who are living: (a) in an institution, perhaps detained under a section of the Mental Health Act 1983, or (b) in the community.

Each of these settings will have its own set of social rules and values, expectations and perhaps even prejudices. It is therefore worth acknowledging that there will be both costs and benefits of treating clients in either setting. The costs, or potential problems, are outlined below. The benefits are the opposite of the costs and are therefore not listed.

The limitations of the social environment of institutional settings have been noted by Black, Cullen and Novaco (1997) and Taylor (2002).

Potential problems of working within an institution

- During initial assessment, clients may not disclose the full extent of their anger and aggression because of shame, or in case it results in perceived risks and hence increased staff observation or restrictions.
- Clients may have a deep sense of mistrust of members of staff because they will be seen as part of a powerful system. Davis and Boster (1992) point out that the client has to learn to trust and not fear the clinician, but in a secure residential setting clinicians do not fully trust clients and clients do not fully trust clinicians. Consequently it may take longer to establish therapeutic alliance (see page 30).
- Clients detained under a section of the Mental Health Act will feel disempowered and naturally this will affect the balance in the collaborative relationship.

- The delicate balance between the needs of the clients, therapeutic requirements and security needs (Renwick et al. 1997) can mean that the therapist may feel that he or she cannot please both the client and the institutional staff.
- It can be difficult for clients to attempt to practise new skills in an environment that is rife with undue provocations. The interactions between clients can be unpredictable, to say the least, and may not reinforce the practice of a new skill. If a client discovers that others do not respond to an assertive request, he or she may resort to his or her previous pattern of aggression.
- Provocative interactions need not be confined to clients. Staff's attitudes and behaviours may well seem provocative particularly if they do not have adequate understanding of the client's needs (Levey and Howells 1991, McDonnell, Reeves, Johnson and Lane 1998). An example is the style and speed that information needs to be delivered (Kevan 2003). Hence staff training and communication with the team, particularly the client's keyworker and team, are essential.
- The physical environment of a locked ward (i.e. lack of privacy and peace) may not be conducive to practising arousal reduction techniques.
- It can be difficult to carry out the application training, or third stage of the treatment (see page 17) when clients are living in a restricted environment. They may not have access to the provocations that were high on their original hierarchical list and hence will not be able to practise their new ways of coping.
- It is very important how the sessions are regarded, both by those who attend and also by fellow clients, members of the treatment team, family, carers or any other people who have influence on the client. As Feindler (1991) states, 'it is important to continue to ensure that it is *not* perceived as a punitive group for trouble makers'.

Potential problems of working in a community setting

- It can be difficult to make direct observational records to back up any self-report data.
- Relatives may have entrenched ill-informed attitudes or behaviours that do not encourage any gradual changes that the client makes.

- The therapist or team may find it difficult to give support between sessions.
- It can be difficult to reinforce new learning and use of techniques.
- How can one give a prompt to do homework? Design a strategy with the client, e.g. stickers on the fridge, or set the phone alarm.
- There is not a captive audience at the Centre where the treatment is delivered. Clients' attendance can be erratic due to their poor memory or executive skills, or their dependence on transport.

FACILITIES

- A suitable group room with comfortable chairs.
- Whiteboard and pens.
- Supply of writing materials/clipboards.
- Visual aids as mentioned in the manual.
- Video equipment – VCR and camcorder.

Key point

For the management of anger to be successful, it is important that individuals engage fully in treatment. This can present a conflict if the treatment has been prescribed for the person by the team and yet the person still regards his or her anger as a benefit rather than a cost to himself or herself. Cultivate an atmosphere that is relaxing and friendly. It is not easy for many people to focus on their anger and resulting behaviours, which may lead to loss of control, fear or guilt. Therefore, the more conducive the setting is to participation, the better. Promote a sense of privilege about being in the sessions; it is not suitable for everyone, but only those who are willing to work hard at learning to 'be boss of' their anger.

Safety precautions

Not suprisingly, clients who attend managing anger sessions have a propensity to become angry, and therapists may feel that they are an unpredictable group to work with. This could potentially cause the therapist alarm, and inhibit the treatment process. Therefore, it is both advisable and reassuring to have in place a number of strategies to provide security to both the therapist and the clients. Discuss these as part of the introduction session.

- Agree, with clients, a plan of action that can be used if they become agitated, i.e. if clients become aware of their own increasing levels of arousal they may leave the session and 'take 5' before returning to continue. As already stated, it is likely that as high levels of arousal are recounted, clients may become agitated. During the early part of the treatment the 'take 5' routine may be the only coping strategy the clients have. Explain to those outside the treatment room that people may need to leave and 'take 5'. Ask that they monitor the person's behaviour but not question or urge them to return to the session. If this becomes too regular the therapist will need to reconsider the person's suitability for the group.

- Let it be known what response will be made if the worst scenario (aggression) is shown. Have an agreed strategy that will be implemented. Depending on the treatment setting there may be an existing procedure that could be used if a client, or clients, become disturbed.

It is wise for the therapist to be aware of de-escalation techniques described on page 35.

STARTING THE PROCESS

ASSESSMENT AND EVALUATION

Effective assessment and evaluation of treatment can be carried out only if adequate information is collected. This involves setting up a system for collecting data from a variety of sources. If this is established before treatment begins, there will then be a framework in place for collecting baseline data and measuring any future change. Four methods of data collection are described below. This is followed by some suggestions for the methods that can be used for pre-treatment (baseline data) collection, the ongoing collection and post-treatment data collection.

Methods of data collection

1. Archival records

This is information on incidents of aggression and outbursts of anger; it can be obtained from case notes or incident reports.

2. Semi-structured interview

A semi-structured interview can elicit a great deal of useful and necessary pre-treatment information. If self-report measures can be used they can be delivered as part of this interview. It is probable that the therapist's assistance maybe needed to administer these (O'Neill 1995, Novaco and Taylor 2004) to compensate for the patient's reading, language and spatial skills; or the dense presentation of the scales.

The components covered in the interview (see page 63) are based on Novaco's model of anger. During this interview process the therapist is able to appreciate more fully the client's awareness of emotions, insight and likelihood of engagement, which is the essential first step of the collaborative process.

3. Self-report measures

Self-report measures are used because anger is a subjective emotion and therefore cannot accurately be reported on by anyone other than the person experiencing it. Self-report measures, such as: the State-Trait Anger Expression Inventory – STAXI (Spielberger 1988); the Novaco Anger Scale and Provocation Inventory – NAS-PI (Novaco 1994a, 2003); Buss–Perry Aggression Questionnaire (Buss and Perry 1992); or the Children's Anger Response Checklist CARC (Feindler et al. 1993, cited in Feindler 1995), have been traditionally used before commencing anger management treatment.

However, reference must be made to the vulnerabilities of self-report measures, not least with a subject who has cognitive impairment. First, the existing measures were not originally validated with this population and, second, the subject's language and literacy skills may pose problems. Nevertheless, Stenfert Kroese (1997) illustrates that people with learning disabilities can self-report. Novaco and Taylor's work (2004) with male offenders who have developmental disabilities, demonstrated high internal consistency between modified versions of the STAXI and the NAS. The self-reported anger was also significantly related to staff records of assaultive behaviour.

Diaries kept during treatment will also provide a valuable source of data. This is, of course, dependent on the client's literacy skills and motivation, but pictorial diaries can overcome this hurdle (see examples in Appendix 2)

4. Direct observational recording

This is the most objective and comprehensive assessment strategy. It is completed by those having most contact with the client and can be used successfully to record overt behaviours such as any aggression. It cannot, however, be used with success to record the subjective emotional state of anger itself, although cognitions may be voiced – *I always get the blame* – and can be recorded.

Because many clients referred for anger treatments have problems with aggression, direct observational recording is relevant and is an invaluable and reliable source of behavioural data. Suitable methods of recording are:

- straightforward ABC, Antecedent, Behaviour, Consequence, charts (described very clearly by Murphy and Clare 1991)
- an 'in-house' behavioural recording sheet;

- a behavioural inventory, such as the OAS-MNR, Overt Aggression Scale Modified for Neurorehabilitation which has been shown to be a reliable method of recording the type and severity of aggression. (Alderman, Knight and Morgan 1997). Any antecedents and interventions used in the management are also noted.
- The Ward Anger Rating Scale (WARS), a two-part observational scale completed by members of staff who know the patient well (Novaco 1994a, Taylor, DuQueno and Novaco 2004)

To ensure reliability of such recording it is necessary for observers to have adequate training both on the rationale of the recording and the technique itself.

Pre-treatment gathering of information

If it is decided that the individual is suitable for treatment, you should collect baseline data. This will allow the measurement of change by:

- archival records
- self-report measures
- diaries. Howells (1989) suggests asking clients, and a significant other, to collect data for two weeks before treatment commences
- direct observational recording, e.g. ABC charts, OAS-MNR or the WARS
- semi-structured interview (see page 63)
- biofeedback to monitor levels of physiological arousal.

Gathering this will contribute to the therapist's understanding of the client and assist treatment planning to include individual needs.

Ongoing collection of data

Feindler and Ecton (1986) describe clearly the need for this. Specific target behaviours can be clearly defined and data collected on incidents of aggression or angry outbursts from:

- the client's case notes
- oral self-report or diaries; the style of diary may change as treatment progresses

- direct observational recording (DOR) using an 'in-house' recording sheet, ABC charts, the OAS-MNR or WARS
- physiological measures, e.g. pulse rate or blood pressure before and after relaxation, or biofeedback to assist self-monitoring of arousal levels.

These data are relatively easy to collect in an institutional setting where staff are primed to observe and record. In other settings, family members or carers may be willing to use simple recording methods to back up self-report data.

Evaluation of treatment

At the end of treatment, data comparable to that collected pre-treatment should be collected. Comparison of the data will provide simple quantitative statistics. Bellack and Hersen (1984) offer information on single case study designs and on group evaluations.

SEMI-STRUCTURED INTERVIEW

The purpose of the semi-structured interview is to:

- gain further understanding of the individual's patterns of anger
- assess the person's degree of self-awareness, acceptance and general attitude towards his or her anger
- highlight an individual's desire or reluctance to manage his or her anger
- raise interest in future treatment
- establish the first step of collaborative work.

Style

The style of the interview is very important. People with anger problems are often feeling resentful, shameful, anxious and/or resistant. Motivational Interviewing techniques, which are designed to help people resolve mixed feelings about change, may be helpful (Miller and Rollnick 2002, Prochaska, DiClemente and Norcross 1992).

Ask open questions, *How? what? where? when?*

Reaffirm – *You seem to have a number of problems to cope with.*

Summarise – *So you say that it is understandable that you get angry, but that you do feel bad afterwards.*

The 5 general principles of Motivational Interviewing are:

1) Express empathy – aim to understand without judging.

2) Develop discrepancy, or dissonance, between the person's present behaviour and their broader goals. Tune yourself to hearing any self-motivational statements and repeat or affirm: *You say most of the time your temper is fine but that sometimes it causes you problems….*

3) Avoid argument, do not push the person into defending his/her behaviour: *No you don't have to change, but I'm thinking about how happy and pleasant you seem when you are calm.*

4) Roll with any resistance, new perspectives are invited not imposed: *You don't have a problem – so tell me how things are for you?*

5) Promote the belief in the possibility of change and support self-efficacy – i.e. the patient chooses and implements change: *Changing is difficult, but you sound a strong person who would work on their goal to be in charge of their anger.*

The interview

- Clarify the reason for the meeting, the background of the referral and explain your role as therapist.
- Explain that anger is a perfectly normal emotion but that we often do not understand it properly. Different people will get angry over different things; it is not the same for everyone. Sometimes getting angry can cause problems for us or others. Ask, '*Would you agree with that?*'
- Sometimes people need some helpful tips on managing their anger. Refer to managing anger sessions (the client may know that others attend).
- Ask if you can try to understand what it is like for the client.

Establish awareness and pattern of anger

The following questions are suggested; they are not prescriptive. It may also be helpful to refer to examples of situations such as those rated highly on the Novaco Provocation Inventory.

You may then elicit genuine responses from the client.

- What are some of the things that make you angry?
- What might make you very angry? And just a little bit angry? (Can client grade degree of anger?)
- Can you tell me what it's like for you when you get angry?
- Have you felt angry recently?
- When was that? Can you tell me about it?
- How often would you say you get angry? (establish frequency).
- Do you get any warning signs? So what might happen?
- Would other people know that you were getting angry? How might they tell?

Body

- When you are angry are you aware of changes in your body? Does it get tense or unsettled? Where in particular? Does this last for long?
- Is your sleep affected?
- How does your body feel after you have been angry? (headaches etc.)

Thoughts

- Does getting angry change the way you think? (can't concentrate, think hateful thoughts, set expectations of others/self?)
- Do you think a lot about what made you angry? (rumination)
- Does that go on for a long time? (duration)

Behaviour

- What might you do when you are angry? (shout, slam, smash things, sulk, self-harm?)
- Would you do different things in different places, or with different people, i.e. at home with family versus strangers or workmates?

Influences

- Are there some places where you are more likely to get angry?
- Are there some places where you are less likely to get angry?

- Does it make any difference who is there?
- What might make it worse? (conditions – heat, noise, hunger)
- What can you do to calm yourself down? Does that always help?
- Do you know of anything else that might help?
- Do you think you get angry more or less often than other people?

Costs/benefits

- So how do you view your anger? (distress; fear; great, no problem!)
- Does it get you what you want?
- Does it get you into trouble?
- How do you feel after you have been angry?
- What do your friends and family think of it?
- What do they say when you get angry?
- Would it be worth trying to learn more skills so that you can be in charge of your anger?
- What would you gain?
- Would your life be very different if you did not get angry as much? Can you think of ways that you could lose out? (concern about changing)

If yes, ask the last question:

- Why, what might happen?

Plan for future treatment

As a result of the pre-treatment gathering of information and the semi-structured interview, the therapist has to decide if the client is ready to commence treatment immediately. It may be decided that the individual would benefit from some pre-sessional work aimed at increasing emotional awareness and self-awareness (see page 68). If the client appears reluctant to see the reason for the treatment, the use of motivational interviewing methods (Miller and Rollnick 2002) may be helpful. Manchester and Wood (2001) illustrate the particular need for collaboration rather than confrontation when working with clients who are reluctantly discovering the effects their brain injury has on emotional regulation.

If the client does seem ready to commence treatment, which format would be most suitable for their needs:

- group sessions?
- individual sessions?
- group plus some individual to 'top up' the cognitive work?
- how many? Agree initial number and review later.

Always involve the client in the negotiation so as to work collaboratively.

PRE-SESSIONAL WORK

Experience has shown that when working with clients with complex needs it may be necessary to include pre-sessional work before commencing the course of anger treatment. This has a number of advantages that enable:

1) Increased emotional identification or recognition.
2) Use of Motivational Interviewing methods (see page 63) to increase client's motivation to learn new ways of coping.
3) Lay the foundations of working in a CBT style and introduce the principles of self-monitoring, rating emotions and relaxation techniques.
4) Opportunity for development of a therapeutic alliance, and if in a group setting, trust between members.

As stated on pages 13 and 48, Novaco's recent work includes a preparatory phase as an integral part of his treatment protocol.

However, when anger is one of many exaggerated emotions, a pre-course module covering the normality of emotions, and the need to regulate them sometimes, is helpful. Clients have responded well to such modules which we have renamed: Coping with Emotions, The Coping Crowd, Aaaaarh Management, or Dealing with Feelings (Lowther Adolescent Unit).

Increasing awareness of emotions

It is very common for clients to have difficulty in recognising and encoding emotions. Most of us are able to identify a range of emotions well before school age. However, learning disability, acquired brain injury, or very disturbed early years may lead to a deficit in emotional recognition and social cognition. When a client experiences an intense feeling of emotion yet cannot understand its meaning, or how to label it, it is no wonder that they are not able to regulate the emotion or express it effectively and with dignity.

Hence, being able to recognise and label emotions both in oneself and others, is central to anger treatments. So for those who need extra time to develop emotional awareness, the following ideas may be useful:

- Look at photographs of famous people depicting various emotions. Sorting cards or pictures of a range of scenarios into piles, e.g. pleasant versus unpleasant emotions.
- Take photographs of the clients showing various emotions.
- Watch videos of television soaps – these usually contain a great deal of emotion! This will help to assess the client's labelling of emotion and their interpretation of events.
- For those who find drawing an easier way to express themselves try books such as Draw on your Emotions (Sunderland and Engleheart 1994).
- Learning tools such as the Emotion Trainer (www.emotiontrainer.co.uk).

Discuss the different words that people use to describe emotions. There may be variations in language depending upon age, and cultural background. Session 1 includes the semantics of anger, and how it differs from aggression, but preparatory work may be needed to clarify the meaning of 'angry type words' versus other emotional words. People may have very different views of the value or need for the varying emotions. For example, anger may be viewed negatively, whereas anxiety, on the other hand, may command tolerance and sympathy. Encourage clients to analyse what they saw by asking questions such as:

- Who was angry/sad/happy?
- Why do you think he/she is angry/sad/happy?
- How angry/sad/happy do you think they are? Start to introduce the concept of measuring emotions. Keep it simple at this stage, e.g. a lot or a little.
- What do you think he/she is feeling in his/her body?
- I wonder what he/she might be thinking?
- What might happen to him/her as a result of getting angry/sad/happy?

Explain that it is possible to experience more than one emotion at any one time, for example sadness and anger. The emotion may also quickly change, say from anxiety to anger; this happens when the arousal becomes relabelled as a result of the thoughts changing.

THE WAY THE MANUAL WORKS

The manual has been designed as a working document for use by fellow therapists and health professionals. The material is copyright, but permission is granted for the user to photocopy the pages indicated for use with clients only. No other parts of this document may be reproduced without the written consent of the author. If information is referred to for any purpose other than treatment sessions, the author requests that reference be given to the document.

Although some background information has been given at the beginning of the manual, further reading is suggested. References for the text and those of additional interest are contained at the end of the manual.

The natural sequence of the three stage stress inoculation anger control treatment will be followed in the manual. However, the rate of progress originally suggested has been amended to suit the needs of those clients with limited cognitive ability. As explained earlier, the three stages – cognitive preparation, skill acquisition phase and application training – are, in practice, interrelated within the treatment sessions. The first part of training actually starts with assessment and the semi-structured interview. It also includes any pre-sessional work to increase emotional awareness, should this be necessary before establishing, and learning about, the individual's pattern of anger. Therefore, the background information about anger has to be passed on to the client *before* the skill training begins. With this group of individuals the trick is to impart that information whilst being mindful that 'chalk and board' techniques may not be effective.

Hence the standard delivery has been adapted. Rather than three distinct phases, the first seven session plans concentrate on the cognitive preparation, and the rest on skill acquisition and application training. It is important to remember that although session plans are numbered, there may be considerable variation in the rate of progress when working through the course. It could be necessary to take more than one session to cover a plan. For this reason, it may be helpful to view each plan as a block rather than as an individual session. The frequency of sessions is not prescribed. In practice, one per week is commonplace, although experience and research has shown that for some clients more frequent sessions may be more effective. For the purpose of this manual, sessions will be referred to as occurring weekly.

Each session plan/outline is presented in a consistent format:

- feedback
- practical work
- relaxation
- homework.

Additional theoretical knowledge on the topic is provided in 'Therapist's Notes'.

Speech is denoted by the use of italics. Examples would be statements or questions used by the therapist, or self-instructional speech used as a result of anger arousal.

For the benefit of the therapist, the early session plans include a good deal of explanation, and as a consequence are considerably longer than later ones.

Also included in the manual are:

- plans for additional sessions, if extra learning/practice is required
- additional information on arousal reduction methods
- resources for use in sessions – hand-outs
- diaries
- worksheets – there are two versions of each, a blank to be used by the client and a completed worksheet to be used as a teaching aid or prompt by the therapist
- feedback sheets.

SESSIONS

SESSION 1

Welcome

Introduce the therapists and members of the group to each other. If the members have already worked together, for example in emotional awareness sessions, the process of meeting for a session will be familiar. Explain that the sessions will focus on anger and how to manage it. Allow members to express their hopes and fears about the sessions whilst maintaining a feeling of respect and optimism.

A cup of tea or coffee can be an inviting extra incentive to attend.

Introduction

To introduce the idea of managing our anger the therapist may say:

Anger is just one of many emotions that we feel.
Do we all get angry at times? Maybe we call it something else.

- Allow the group to suggest other words for anger: rage, mad, pissed off, furious, wound-up, 'on your toes', etc.
- Compare the likelihood of getting angry with that of getting anxious, afraid or other normal emotions.

Practical

Let's find out what makes us angry.

Divide into two groups and work with a large sheet of paper to brainstorm – *what makes us angry*? Examples are given in the box.

WHAT MAKES US ANGRY?

Not being able to do what I want
People taking the mickey
Being hurt
People not understanding what I'm trying to say
Not being able to think what to say
Messing up, or not doing things properly
Being accused of something I didn't do
People staring at me
Busy places and people getting in our way
Queuing or waiting
Memories
People referring to my bad past

Note: some of these anger triggers are human errors, for example losing or forgetting things. We all suffer from these at times, but for those with cognitive dysfunction, such errors are more likely. Members may be too proud or reluctant to acknowledge them.

(Keep the sheet of paper to refer to later)

At this stage there may be a great deal of confusion between the internal state or feeling of anger and the behaviours associated with aggression. Explain the difference briefly if necessary, but this will be clarified later. Do not issue too much theory in any one session, particularly the first.

Feedback

Draw out that perhaps we do all get angry and that it is quite normal to get angry sometimes.

> This is necessary because many people feel it is wrong to get angry. They may associate anger with behaviours for which they

have been scolded or punished, and consequently have learned to relabel or deny the feeling until the anger arousal is out of control.

But anger can have a **bad** side if, as a result of it, we:

- do or say things we regret
- hurt others or ourselves
- get into trouble
- are seen as a risk and so not included in things
- lose friends
- feel bad about ourselves.

So can the effects last longer than the anger?

Explain

1. These sessions will help to teach us what to do when we feel angry so that we can remain in charge of the anger, rather than allowing the anger to take us over.
2. The sessions are **NOT** about taking the anger away; we all need it sometimes to tell us that things are not right or that there is a problem to solve. Give examples, such as someone going into your room to steal something, being threatened or hurt. Refer to some other justifiable causes of anger that were given in the brainstorming exercise and use them as examples.
3. The sessions are about learning to see anger as a 'warning sign' on which to take a different action. Introduce the 'take 5' routine (see page 55) to use as a response to arrest increasing arousal levels.

Note: These points may need to be reiterated regularly in sessions.

Stress the one important rule in the group:

NO VIOLENCE

Therapists need to decide on a strategy that will be followed if there is any physical aggression shown. The priority is to maintain a safe environment. It may be necessary to stop proceedings and request that the individuals involved leave the group; or, separate the antagonists, distract the group from the disruption, and continue with the session. Do not discuss the incident until the person has had a cooling down period, then, if he or she is willing, try to establish the reason for the upset and consider if there were alternative ways of reacting.

Expectations

Finish by explaining the expectations of the group, that each week:

- we shall all attend sessions, and specify the time, say 40 minutes or one hour long
- we shall do practical work in small groups
- if the hope is to use video recording then make it sound fun. Ask if people have used it before and confirm that you will only use it with their permission. Consult the local consent policy.
- members will practise what they have learned in a session – use the word 'homework' if that seems appropriate
- there will be contact with the individual's key worker if applicable
- we shall finish with a 'winding down', relaxing time.

By the end of this session it is hoped that the group will:

- have enjoyed the session!
- intend to come next week (commitment)
- have some understanding of what will be expected of them
- have heard of the normality of anger as well as the problems associated with it.

Therapist's notes

Anger is very personal, and different for each of us; it depends on an individual's standards, attitudes and beliefs (see Novaco model cited in O'Neill 1995). Often the current event that triggers the anger response is linked to our past memories (old tapes), as well as our beliefs and expectations about what 'should' and 'ought' to happen.

The exercise in this session helps both the individual concerned and the therapist learn about the individual's patterns of anger, in readiness to spot potential triggers in future.

SESSION 2

Welcome

Recap

In last week's session we agreed:

- that we all get angry sometimes
- that some of us call it something else
- that different things make us angry (it may be useful to produce the brainstorming list from last week's session as a reminder)
- anger is a normal emotion, but it can have a bad side
- how the sessions will help us
- expectations of the group.

Practical

Now work towards learning what people **DO** when they are angry. Brainstorm ideas – examples may be, shout, throw things, clench fists, hit people or the wall, mutter, make rude signs, swear, sulk, run away, self-harm, pace around. Hopefully there will be some adaptive behaviours suggested as well. Create clusters, or a continuum, on the board, hence highlighting the differences between unacceptable physical aggression, verbal aggression and acceptable, even helpful, ways of behaving such as leaving the situation or being assertive.

- Now clarify the difference between anger and aggression (see below).
- Refer to the brainstorming ideas, and pull out a few examples of anger and aggression to illustrate the point.

ANGER	is an emotion that we 'feel', when we believe that something is wrong. It's personal and can't really be seen by others. It might make us feel ready to act and then we have a choice, if, when, and how we do so.
AGGRESSION	on the other hand, is different. It is the 'doing part' that others can see, hear or feel, and therefore report on. It is not acceptable and can lead to trouble and/or pain to others or ourselves.

Now the therapist may ask:

- *do they always go together?*
- *does anger always lead to aggression?*
- *do we have to be angry to be aggressive?*

Give examples of occasions where aggression is not necessarily caused by anger; for example, football hooligans who throw and smash things along with the crowd, or indeed how any of us could show instrumental aggression without being angry. The therapist may wish to give an example of this by dashing into the room, banging the furniture about and throwing things. He or she could then explain that he or she was not angry but wanting a response! This is also good as an icebreaker!

- *So you don't have to be angry to be aggressive.*
- *Some people have just learned that aggression pays off!*
- *It gets them what they want – or does it?*

Discuss

NOT ALL AGGRESSION IS CAUSED BY ANGER

AND ANGER NEED NOT LEAD TO AGGRESSION

Aggressive behaviour is learned and it can also be unlearned. There is a choice, and these sessions will teach us skills so that we have a choice of ways to behave when angry.

Relaxation/arousal reduction

So today we have shown how being ANGRY, *FIZZING*, BOILING *'winds us up' and so we must learn how to wind down!*

But how do we know if we are successful? How do we measure?

- Introduce the 'anger thermometer' (see Appendix 1, page 179) as a visual way of grading how angry we are. A large cardboard version is a helpful tool, which can be referred to during sessions.
- Explain the analogy of 'boiling up' or 'being cool' to anger and calm.
- Ask each person to estimate where he or she is currently on the scale (level of arousal). The accuracy of this is likely to improve as a person learns to experience how it feels to be relaxed. Only then can they really grade their level of arousal.
- Now begin the habit of finishing the session by using simple relaxation techniques, start with calming breaths (see Appendix 1, page 167).

We are often told to keep calm, but how do we do that?

A good way is to take control of our breathing. This will help us to:

- reduce any body tension
- concentrate on something apart from what is making us angry
- give us time to think before we speak or shout!

Now where are you on the thermometer? Any change?

Praise or encourage as necessary.

Homework

Introduce the idea of self-monitoring in between sessions. The goal is to:

- record how many times they got angry in a day/week
- record the intensity on a scale of 0–100
- grade your expectations according to the members' ability

- some clients may ultimately prefer to design their own scale (more on this in session 6).

Practise how to do the homework. Inform and involve relevant staff so as to gain their support and practical help. Provide each client with a folder so that they can keep their personal data (diaries, hand-outs, coping strategies, etc.) and feel a sense of ownership in the treatment.

Therapist's notes on self-monitoring

In general, people are not in the habit of monitoring their behaviour or feelings, and therefore self-monitoring is a task that is foreign to most. It is a complex pattern of behaviour and involves recognition and awareness of the behaviour or emotion to be monitored, as well as the recording process itself. Both of these aspects may lead to problems, and individuals may need to be trained both to discriminate and record incidents of anger arousal.

Yet self-monitoring is intrinsic to treatment, and a necessary monitoring device for recording incidents of anger, which is a subjective emotion, and can be accurately reported on only by the individual concerned. The act of self-recording can be an intervention in its own right (Pope and Jones 1996). For if it raises awareness of the anger, so that recordings can be made; this can, in turn, influence the sequence of events. So if possible try to encourage at least some degree of self-monitoring, which should develop increased self-awareness. There is great scope for creativity and ingenuity when devising a recording system for patients with poor literacy skills, e.g. wrist counters, 'making a mark' on a picture of an angry person, putting a symbol on a chart, moving a button or a counter from one pocket to another each time there is an incident of anger arousal and then counting up at the end of a given period (staff assistance may be needed).

Diaries help to build up a picture of anger patterns, which allows both the therapist and the individual to learn the potential triggers. They also provide 'real' situations to role-play.

Individuals will need encouragement and help while the habit of self-monitoring develops. Discuss with the participants when and how they will self-monitor and practise the behaviour using role-play. Remember, failure to complete self-monitoring and diaries is often not due to lack of motivation or poor compliance, rather it is expecting a specific skill that has to be learned. Therefore, be encouraging about any recording in order to shape the behaviour.

Note: In order to obtain objective feedback of behaviours and to measure change, it is also wise to make observational recordings (see page 60).

SESSION 3

Welcome

Check homework and feedback

- Ask if anyone kept a record of the frequency and/or the intensity of their anger incidents.
- Praise **ANY** recording, be encouraging! (keep records).
- Start to develop the habit of each person reporting on incidents of anger. Refer to any self-monitoring, if it is available, or rely on oral feedback if not. In this case you may like to fill in the diary during this session.

There are obvious weaknesses in self-reporting, whether written or oral, but it is an important part of the training and self-monitoring. It is helpful to try to cultivate a setting in which individuals feel they can report back honestly without judgement being passed or fear of any consequences.

Clients may report incidents very differently to staff recordings. Do not overtly challenge this in public; the discrepancy reflects poor monitoring skills, unrealistic expectations, or face-saving denial. Instead, acknowledge that that is the client's interpretation, and when relevant, try and pose the question that the incident might have seemed or felt different to others:

You say you didn't hit him but you felt very angry, do you think he would known that by the look on your face?

- Encourage reports from each person on incidents that:
  - they handled well, i.e. started to feel arousal but managed to keep control
  - became aroused, angry and/or aggressive, and lost control.
- Offer praise for the former and support/reassurance/optimism for the latter!
- Try to be encouraging and positive. Remember, anger is often associated with poor self-esteem. Anger may be accompanied by feelings of punishment and guilt; it is important that a firm yet optimistic attitude is fostered to encourage honesty and co-operation.

Recounting incidents of anger may lead to arousal. If this is the case use it as an 'on the spot' opportunity to a) self monitor, b) use calming breaths and c) compare level of arousal.

Recap

Recap on the main points of last week's session:

- that people may **DO** different things when they are angry
- the difference between anger and aggression, or the feeling and the behaviours
- how the two relate (remembering that aggression is **not** acceptable).

It is important to start to get the message across that, despite provocation and even if we are stressed, we still have a responsibility to behave in a socially acceptable way. Our behaviour can make a situation worse, inflame it or calm it.

Discuss

Is it always a bad thing to get angry? Can it ever be a good thing? Brainstorm ideas, examples are given in the box below. Consider the good and the bad points.

Brainstorm

Good points/benefits

- gives us energy
- makes us deal with things
- provides a sense of control
- makes us brave enough to say something we wanted to
- saves face – it's easier than admitting you are wrong!
- gives others a message that they need to watch it
- raises our sense of justice

Bad points/costs

- hurts others/self
- loses us friends/lonely
- we can't think or reason
- we get into trouble
- we say things we later regret
- it creates a bad atmosphere
- we feel awful, guilty, weak or embarrassed
- we worry how others will be with us when we next see them
- we can't sleep and keep thinking about it

Appendix 1 refers to the effects of anger arousal on cognitive skills and performance. This is relevant to all of us, but particularly to those who have cognitive impairments.

Introduce

- the idea that although there are some things that would anger most people, for example having a personal possession stolen, often an event will not anger us all to the same degree, or even at all.
- ways of collecting more information on each individual's anger triggers and form a hierarchy of provocations. This can be kept in a client's folder and added to as triggers are discovered through self-monitoring and recordings. Novaco (1993–4) suggests using index cards to record anger experiences, and grading the degree of anger experienced. Clearly, clients will need help with this process, but these anger hierarchies can be used later when new skills are applied and practised in progressively more difficult situations (this is the application training stage of the stress inoculation treatment).

So we are beginning to learn that each of us may get angry because of different things. We are also going to keep records of our own anger triggers and high-risk times. This will help us understand our personal patterns of anger.

Now look at the hierarchies or brainstorming list from Session 1, and consider:

- Do these things always make you angry in the same way?
- What affects our anger?

Ask the group to suggest ideas, such as:

- *how we were when we woke up – grumpy?*
- *what else has gone wrong*
- *who said 'that annoying remark' to us*
- *how noisy it is*
- *how well we slept*
- *had we eaten?*
- *drugs, alcohol*
- *large amounts of caffeine (coffee, caffeinated drinks)*
- *pain or bodily discomfort*
- *fatigue (particularly relevant to brain-injured clients)*

Use examples to illustrate this idea.

But we can prevent some of these things; or at least be aware of them and of their effects and then make adjustments. Introduce the idea of 'the P words' (see Appendix 2, page 209) – planning, preparing and pacing which may help avoid tiredness and fatigue after a busy event. Talk about the need to adjust the environment to avoid irritation and anger arousal. Explain that our bodies like routine and so it is important to eat, sleep and exercise regularly.

This is all part of taking responsibility and being in charge of our own anger.

Homework

Continue self-monitoring. Repeat the method used or adjust as necessary.

Relaxation/arousal reduction

Let's look at the thermometer before we start.
Continue with calming breaths or step 1 of OTSAR (see Appendix 1, page 167). Promote their use:

- calming breaths are easy to use
- you don't need a relaxation mat or any special equipment
- they can be done anywhere, at any time.

Anyone feel more calm and less tense?

Therapist's notes

Breathing and relaxation are a vital part of anger control. When we are angry or anxious our bodies pump out adrenaline. This, in turn, is likely to lead to fast, shallow breathing and alters the balance of oxygen and carbon dioxide circulating in the blood. If this imbalance is not corrected, it can stimulate further release of adrenaline and lead to even more anger or stress. Therefore, taking control of this snatched breathing by forcing a slower, deeper and regular pattern of breathing can hinder the effects of the excess adrenaline. The result should be an increased sense of calmness and control and, therefore, a greater chance of future behaviour being based on judgement, rather than on impulse.

Hence, breathing is a key part of '**O**n **T**he **S**pot **A**rousal **R**eduction' or OTSAR. It is therefore the first step of OTSAR, the method of which will be gradually introduced along with self-statements as a quick technique to 'take the edge off' the level of arousal. It can complement full relaxation, or be an alternative, user-friendly, coping device (see Appendix 1 for information on OTSAR).

SESSION 4

Welcome

Check homework

- *Did anyone do any self-monitoring, or measure their mercury level?*
- Give praise if they did, but remember it may take a while to establish the habit.
- *Where are you now on the thermometer scale?*

Feedback

Ask about each person's week, both the situations that ended well and those that were a problem (staff input may be useful here).

This process helps to:

- establish the normality of anger
- discourage denial of getting angry
- raise awareness of monitoring self
  are any patterns emerging? e.g. worse if hungry, fatigued, etc.
- establish some support/understanding within the group.

> BUT BEWARE OF GLORIFICATION OF INCIDENTS AND ENSURE REPORTING IS NOT AN OPPORTUNITY TO CRITICISE OTHERS

Recap

- on previous theory of anger versus aggression
- the good and bad points of anger

- that things around us affect our anger.

We said that anger may lead us to **DO** different things (change our behaviour) but that is not the only way anger changes us.

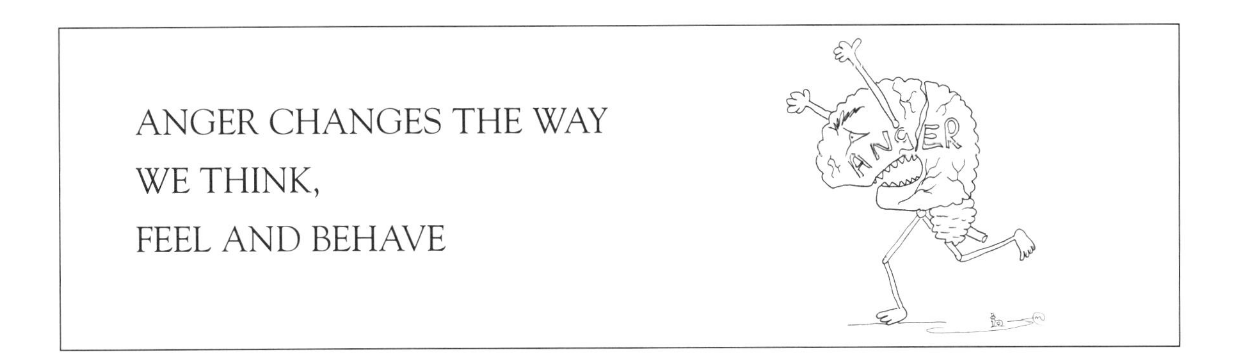

ANGER CHANGES THE WAY
WE THINK,
FEEL AND BEHAVE

Practical

This week we shall think about how it changes our bodies (the feeling part).

- Ask for a volunteer to lie on the floor on a large sheet of paper and draw around them. If this is not appropriate, provide a printed sheet such as the 'outline of a person' worksheet found in Appendix 1 (page 185).
- Then divide into two small groups (with a member of staff in each) and brainstorm what happens to your body when you are angry, i.e. heart rate and breathing quickens, muscles tense, red face, etc.
- Re-form into a large group to give feedback, and mark the changes on the paper body as they are mentioned. Explain that body arousal is often the first signal that we feel when we begin to feel angry. It is part of the normal 'fight flight' response that we could need one day.
- Discuss all the effects and how the poor old body suffers, e.g. headache, stiff neck, stomach ache, feeling sick, shaky, tired or having a tight chest.

YOUR BODY DESERVES BETTER THAN THIS!
So look after yourself and choose to try and keep calm.

Homework

Continue with self-monitoring, but take notice of the 'feeling part'. Use the 'outline of a person' worksheet (Appendix 1) or a simple diary, as in Appendix 4.

Relaxation/arousal reduction

- *Where are you now on the thermometer scale?*
- Continue practising calming breaths – step 1 of OTSAR (Appendix 1).
- Now introduce step 2 of OTSAR, and allow longer for this procedure.
- Explain and demonstrate the difference between tense and relaxed postures.
- Then allow individuals to try them, using whichever position (sitting or lying down) is most acceptable to them.
- Give feedback on how they looked.
- Ask how they felt (proprioceptive feedback) – *down on the scale?*

Therapist's notes

Tension is an early sign of anger arousal, and so if tension is high we are more easily provoked. Therefore, it is necessary to learn to recognise tension as a WARNING SIGN.

It is important that we are aware of the difference between tensed and relaxed muscles; this can be learned through relaxation training. Once we are able first to self-monitor and then differentiate between the two bodily states, we can choose to take a certain course of action as tension arises. If we are well rehearsed in this action it can be implemented even in quite challenging situations. Any extra relaxation sessions offered in addition to this work will enhance the effect.

Many clients who have acquired a brain injury report that they experience very intense and rapidly rising levels of arousal. They may be fearful of their potential loss of control, which in turn increases the level of anxiety arousal. With this group in particular, it is important to teach them ways of picking up the warning signs, arresting the arousal and adjusting their environment. All of this has to be done before any reasoning is carried out.

SESSION 5

Welcome

Check homework

Praise any recordings.

Feedback

Review any anger arousal since the last session. Look at situations that ended well and those that were a problem.

Ask questions such as:

- *what started it all?* (trigger)
- *what did you do?* (behaviour)
- *was anyone hurt?* (awareness)
- *how did it all end up?* (consequences)
- *did you lose out?* (consequences)
- *did you get into trouble?*(consequences)
- *did your body feel different?* (arousal)
- *was it worth getting angry?*

Recap

Being angry leads us to **think**, **feel** and **behave** differently.

- In the last session we were looking at the body changes (the feeling part). Reproduce the drawing of the body from the last session.
- Remind members of the changes in the body – of the effects on the body and on our health – if we are in a tense state too often, and for too long.

Practical

- Last session we took longer for relaxation and started to learn the difference between tense and relaxed muscles.
- We need to take notice of the tension and treat it as a **warning sign**.

Any ideas about what can we do to calm our body when we get that warning sign? Brainstorm ideas such as:

- taking a long slow deep breath out – get rid of the hot air
- push our shoulders down
- alter posture, e.g. if standing, sit down
- stretch out arms and legs and break the tension
- check fingers are opened out – no fists
- take a slow walk
- visualise someone we admire keeping calm (role model)
- have a cool drink
- take gentle exercise, such as swimming.

Homework

Continue self-monitoring as before, so as to raise awareness of anger arousal.

Relaxation arousal/reduction

Allow longer for this, as in the last session.

Therapist's notes

People often feel that they **must** release the anger from their body by vigorous exercise, or by other substitute activities such as using a punch bag. Whilst punching a punch bag is better than punching another person, caution should be exercised. It is not just a case of getting it out of your system, for the thoughts or cognitions that originally fuelled the anger will not have changed and remain there to do so again unless they are reappraised or challenged.

It is difficult to punch something and have calming thoughts!

Also if a person gets into the habit of releasing anger through punching, what happens when they feel angry but are not near a punch bag?

Therapist's notes (continued)

Yet some individuals do report benefit from participating in vigorous exercise when they are angry. If this is the case, help them to appreciate the process. Exercise does use up some adrenaline and after a period of exercise they may feel tired, less 'fired up' and so more able to reappraise their thoughts. However at other times, vigorous activities may maintain the levels of physiological arousal at a high level. If this arousal is not reduced by calming-down exercises, it may well remain only to transfer to a provoking situation in the near future. This can explain why, at times, a minor annoyance can result in an experience of intense anger.

Encourage clients to have a winding-down period after any vigorous exercise. Try a slow walk with long stretching steps and the arms loosely swinging whilst the breathing returns to a gentle regular pace. This will allow the physiological arousal levels to decline before the individual may encounter another provocation. However, more importantly, encourage them to 'rethink' their anger to see if it was justified and, if so, to voice any grievances calmly.

SESSION 6

Welcome

Check homework

Praise any recording.

Feedback

Check on any anger arousal since the last session.

Recap

- We have been looking at the changes that can take place in our body when we get angry (use our drawing of the body as a prompt).
- *Has anyone felt any of these changes since the last session?*
- Use any discussion as revision.

SO ANGER CAN MAKE OUR BODIES FEEL DIFFERENT!

Let's learn to think of that different feeling as a warning sign
Some people think of it as a **NE-NAR, NE-NAR siren!**

Practical

- Consult the thermometer and make some correlations between mercury levels and increased arousal.
- Suggest there maybe a point where our anger begins to 'take over and really fire us up'. This could be our Ne-Nar zone.

- Allow each person to state their present 'feelings' (level of arousal).

Discuss

Let's test it out. Give an example of an angry situation.

- *Do our feelings change?*
- *Do we go up the thermometer?*

Role-play

- Therapist/therapist or therapist/client, role-play a typical situation that would be provoking to individuals.
- Refer to arousal levels on the thermometer.
- Discuss.

Homework

Continue with self-monitoring (a diary sheet that includes a picture of the thermometer may now be used, see Appendix 4, page 226; add the Ne-Nar zone if applicable).

Relaxation/arousal reduction

- Afterwards, look at the thermometer and rate levels of arousal.

Mention the benefits of keeping calm or below the Ne-Nar zone (see Appendix 1).

Feeling calm before you leave?

Therapist's notes

There is scope to customise the anger thermometer (see example in Appendix 1). Members may like to design their own scale/thermometer, but if not provide one. Any fun measuring scale could be used. Other suggestions are: a kettle (with a lid that blows off at boiling point), a bottle of fizzy pop with a top that could blow, or a volcano (Stallard 2002). Agree which recording sheet will be practical. Discuss where they will keep it or display it as a prompt.

SESSION 7

Welcome

Check homework

Praise any recording.

Feedback

- Check on each person's week, situations that ended well, or not so well.
- Use the thermometer to measure levels of arousal.

Recap

On earlier sessions:

- the changes that take place in our bodies when we start to get angry
- refer to the drawing of the body
- how can we tell if it is happening?
- how might our bodies **FEEL** as we 'boil-up' or go up the thermometer?

Introduce

- the idea that as we get angry our thoughts also change. This concept is hard to grasp for many, so it is introduced in a general way rather than person-specific.

Discuss

- Explore what people may 'think' when they are angry.
- Use the bubble picture (see Appendix 2, page 194) to illustrate the thoughts of an angry person compared with those of a happy contented person.

- Describe two scenarios or role-play scenes around the above point, and discuss the possible resulting behaviours and physiological arousal.
- *Imagine where you would get to on the thermometer ....*
  Thinking about this may have increased your levels of arousal; so let's Breathe OUT slowly and blow away the anger.

Homework

- Continue using the thermometer diary and rate levels of arousal.
- Practise relaxation/arousal reduction techniques.
  Members may like to keep a record of this in their file. Explain the form Relaxation or OTSAR practice (see in Appendix 1); suggest involving 'an-other' and perhaps a visual prompt, to remind or help with the process.

Relaxation/arousal reduction

- Use the thermometer before and after.
- If clients have grasped the difference between tense and relaxed muscles and are beginning to self-monitor when asked to, then step 3 of OTSAR can be introduced.

Therapist's notes

Feindler uses the term trigger to describe the anger-provoking event or antecedent. This could be a direct provocation (verbal, physical or gesture), or an indirect trigger which is associated with the individual's internal appraisal or perception of a situation. If these appraisals are distorted, unhelpful cognitions will be present (e.g. *they are late on purpose just to wind me up*). Current triggers that provoke anger can be linked to the person's past, as well as their expectations and beliefs. We all acquire a collection of 'old tapes' or cognitions that can be triggered by a current event; for example, being shouted at today could set off the 'old tapes' of when parents used to bully us in childhood.

The trigger may be misinterpreted if an individual's information processing is impaired. Having to struggle to extract the meaning of a situation may lead to anxiety, feeling stupid, loss of control, and anger, either at ourselves, or towards others resulting in the need to place the blame externally.

SESSION 8

Therapist's notes

Moving on to the **skill acquisition** and **application training** phases:

It is expected that the assessment, interview, any pre-sessional work and the block of sessions so far, will have completed the **cognitive preparation** work. Therefore, it is hoped that the client will be:

- engaged in treatment
- aware of the costs of their anger
- working, with the therapist, to learn their own patterns of anger
- developing the fundamentals of self-monitoring
- appreciating the components of anger (physiological, behavioural and cognitive)
- interested in learning alternative ways of coping.

This now leads into the **skill training phase**. The **application of skills** is incorporated during this, and during any additional sessions (see page 134) plus follow-up sessions.

Welcome

Check homework

Did anyone try using the relaxation or OTSAR practice sheet? Anyone design a helpful prompt or visual reminder that they would like to share?

Feedback

Reviews on events since the last session.

- Was anyone aware of any changes in their body as they started to get angry?
- Was everyone practising their relaxation/arousal reduction techniques?

Recap

- When we get angry our **thoughts** change and that affects our **bodily feelings** and **behaviour**.

Practical

- Work in pairs and use the 'angry man' bubble picture (see Appendix 2, page 194). Describe an angry scenario and imagine the resulting thoughts. Write them in the bubbles.
- Staff input may be needed in each group.

People often feel that they shouldn't think bad thoughts and so it may be difficult for them to write them down.

Explain

Some thoughts, for example:

- *I want to hurt him*
- *it's not fair*
- *why are they doing this to me?*

are unhelpful and actually help to 'wind us up' which makes the situation worse, whereas others, such as:

- *I need to talk someone and try to sort this out*

might not do so, for they are more helpful and constructive (some say they calm us and act as tranquillisers!).

- Look again at bubble pictures and spot which thoughts are 'wind-up thoughts', and which are not. Mark the unhelpful thoughts to distinguish them from any helpful calming thoughts.
- Use the hand-outs of 'wind-up' and 'helpful calming' thoughts (see Appendix 2, pages 196–199).

NOTE: THIS ASPECT IS DIFFICULT TO GRASP AND WILL TAKE A GREAT DEAL OF REPEATED EXPLANATION. CONSEQUENTLY, MORE TIME IS GIVEN TO IT .

Homework

Use another bubble picture (see Appendix 2, pages 194–195) to record some 'hot', angry thoughts during the week. Staff may need to help if individuals have poor literacy skills, or if they need tactful encouragement to remember incidents! Continue relaxation or OTSAR practice record.

Relaxation/arousal reduction

Describe Step 3 of OTSAR, or your method of preference. Use the thermometer before and after to monitor any changes. We can wind ourselves up, so we need to:

LEARN TO WIND DOWN!

Therapist's notes

Self-statements – the way we think – can affect how we feel in a fairly direct, intentional fashion. We can influence our thoughts by a sort of internal monologue – an ongoing series of statements to ourselves – in which we tell ourselves what to think and believe, and even how to behave (Meichenbaum 1985). These self-statements have a direct effect on physiological symptoms and the decision-making process. Hence, self-statements can either arouse anger or reduce it.

This is the core ingredient when managing anger.

SESSION 9

Welcome

Feedback

Review the week, **but don't look at the homework yet**, we shall use it during the session.

Recap

Recall last week's session.

- Remind ourselves what unhelpful wind-up thoughts are.
- Now look at the homework (decide if it is most appropriate for this to be done quietly with a staff member or in front of the group).
- *Is it becoming clear which are the unhelpful thoughts?*
- Use examples to demonstrate – *would thinking those 'wind-up' thoughts over and over again take you up the anger thermometer?* Perhaps use the third person – *If you saw someone else telling your friend that (the wind-up thoughts) would you think they were unkind?*
- Contrast with a suitable calming, helpful thought and refer to the thermometer again. Examples of coping self-statements are in Appendix 2.

Role-play

- Choose a scene that is familiar to group members, where a person is repeatedly thinking 'wind-up' thoughts. The therapist could then role-play the scene whilst the rest of the group observe any effect on that person's body and behaviour.
- Afterwards, discuss the effect and draw attention to the key points.

EVENT (trigger)	THINK ⟶ FEEL ⟶ DO ⟶

The sequence above can be drawn on a whiteboard as a demonstration, but it is likely that individuals will be able to identify with either end before the middle! They may feel that their behaviour is a powerful automatic response to a trigger.

- Again, make a contrast by repeating the scene when the person is thinking calm, peaceful thoughts.
- Refer to the thermometer.

So do we all experience wind-up thoughts?

Most people do, but are we aware of them? Probably not, they can be automatic, and 'just happen'. We may not pay attention to them because we are too busy thinking what we want to do as a result of the anger.

- Use the Think → Feel → Do sequence hand-outs to illustrate the sequence (see Appendix 2, pages 200–202).

The homework and the sessions aim to help us to learn to notice our 'wind-up' thoughts compared with more helpful calming ones.

Homework

Repeat of bubble pictures or other diaries.

Relaxation/arousal reduction

- Learning to 'wind down'.
- Step 3 of OTSAR.
- Check level on the thermometer afterwards.

Therapist's notes Understanding the cognitive aspects of anger arousal

So far we have established a very simplistic connection between thoughts, emotions (in this case anger) and behaviour. There is much more to the cognitive aspects of anger (explained more fully in Appendix 2), but at present the therapist needs to appreciate that the following influence anger arousal:

1. **Noticing the provocation** in the first place! Some people, more than others, are tuned to notice things that will annoy them. This could mean that their focus of attention shifts towards the potential provocation. This can be a reflection of their past experiences, for example people who have been exposed to confrontation or physical abuse in the past have a tendency to be 'on guard' against further abuse. For them, this may be an adaptive response because it prepares them for a situation that could be interpreted as potentially hurtful.
2. **Expectations** – unrealistic or rigid expectations can 'set us up' for anger. Some people expect trouble, or that the situation will end up in an argument/fight.
3. **Appraisal** – a situation may be perceived as a threat. This automatic process depends on past events (old tapes) as well as on rules and beliefs.
4. **'Wind-up' thoughts** – either verbal or visual, based on the above, can fuel the level of arousal.

So our interpretation of an incident, how we feel it will affect us, and what we say to ourselves all select and govern the emotion we feel.

How much of this aspect can be taught?

As much as the individuals can understand, but point 4 is the most important. Some individuals grasp very little of the cognitive aspects of anger and are able to follow only simple behavioural instructions, i.e. *breathe out, push your shoulders down and walk away!* This of course is a successful way of avoiding a confrontation, but it does not address levels of residual arousal or, more importantly, stop the 'wind-up' thoughts which may lead to future rumination, feelings of inadequacy and further arousal. Others may be able to understand the 'wind-up' process and learn strategies to challenge and re-appraise their biased perception.

Sessions 15–18 will include further cognitive restructuring work for those clients who are able to grasp this aspect of treatment.

SESSION 10

Welcome

Check homework and feedback

Since the last session:

- were any angry thoughts recorded?
- did they fuel an angry situation?
- how was the week?
- is relaxation or OTSAR working?

Recap

On the physiological and cognitive aspects of anger:

- the unhelpful wind-up thoughts
- any resulting changes in the body and behaviour

The THINK ⟶ FEEL ⟶ DO sequence (T ⟶ F ⟶ D)

What might we do as a result of having these thoughts and getting wound up?

Practical

- Brainstorm what people do at present.
- Some examples may be helpful, e.g. listen to music, talk to others, etc., but some will be poor coping skills, e.g. getting wound-up, go up the thermometer, and then become aggressive!

- Naturally, reinforce the adaptive behaviours but also be reassuring and optimistic for those who 'lose it'.

Therapist's notes

By now it is hoped that individuals have some understanding about their anger, and will have acquired the confidence to acknowledge its presence.

Introduce the idea that each of us has a **choice** as to how we behave and has responsibility for our own actions. Too often we let others control how we feel, and then, what we do; so we may even allow them to give us a good or a bad day!

Emotions can become infectious!

We can try to change others' behaviour, but we are often not successful. Yet one thing we CAN have control over is how we react to them. We all enjoy being able to attribute 'what has happened' to somebody, or something, else, for this makes us feel free of responsibility, and it is comfortable. However, these external attributions have to be challenged, without apportioning blame or guilt, to allow the individual to take ownership of their behaviour.

When anger is a valid experience, perhaps after an assault or trauma, a natural grieving process will be necessary before the injustice can be acknowledged and then reappraised. However, if external blame remains as the main focus the person's adjustment will be hampered.

There is a choice of how long we hang on to the blame and anger, before looking forward, don't get stuck, you deserve to move on!
Anger and hate use up energy and that's tiring for you!
So who's in charge? – You or your anger? (See worksheet in Appendix 4, page 241)

In future sessions we will learn how that energy and attention could be put to better use in problem solving, assertion and resolving conflicts.

The concept of having choice may be foreign to those who are dependent upon others and consequently may feel themselves to be 'a victim of the system'.

Yet to spread this message is a way of empowering the individual.

Now suggest that we can learn better ways of coping when we feel that we are beginning to boil up, or to sense the warning signs. Remember, when we are aroused we do not perform well and so 'sell ourselves badly'.
You owe it to yourself to keep calm! (see Appendix 1, page 162)

- Explain that thinking about your anger tends to make it worse, but how can you stop? We need to arrest those thoughts and put them in the bin! (see worksheet and cartoon in Appendix 2). Distraction can be helpful by not letting you pay any attention to your anger – but again, how?

Any ideas of things to ***DO*** *or* ***THINK?***

- Work in pairs or singly, use the worksheet 'Ways To Calm' to record any suggestions that are offered (see Appendix 4, page 236). A completed version is also included for extra ideas.
- Share suggestions and pick out any that could be unhelpful. Reinforce the good ones!
- Keep the sheets, we shall repeat the exercise at a later date to see if there are more ideas.

Homework

Continue with simple diaries (pictorial, if literacy skills are poor). Encourage group members to prompt and support each other with the task.

Relaxation/arousal reduction

By now the technique of **O**n The **S**pot **A**rousal **R**eduction must be coming familiar, and the discipline of 'turning it on' to demand, is hopefully being practised.

- In this session, before starting the procedure, encourage each person to get up and pace around while remembering an anger-provoking situation, then to find a chair, 'plonk themselves in it' and commence the arousal reduction. This is still step 3 of OTSAR.
- Look at the anger thermometer and register the level of arousal before and after.

SESSIONS 11/12

Welcome

Check homework and feedback

Recap

Review the discussion about:

- what people **DO** when they are angry – remember some things were helpful and others were not
- our having a choice and a responsibility for our behaviour
- the list of ideas of what to do or think when getting angry (produce the worksheet from the last session).

So what's going to make us do or think these things ?

Introduce

Self-Instruction Training – the 'think aloud' approach, or things that we say or think to ourselves to remind us to:

- do different actions, e.g. *move away*
- reduce body arousal, e.g. *breathe out, shoulders down*
- question our thoughts, e.g. *maybe he didn't mean it*

This is about learning to follow certain steps to calm down!
But in the heat of an angry moment we may not remember the self-instruction and may need:

REMINDERS!

Show examples of visual or verbal prompts:

- a small pocket-size card
- pages to fit into a coping book
- posters on the bedroom wall may be useful
- recordings of scripts that can be played when anger is escalating
- pictures and messages on phones
- photographs of self breathing out and walking away

Each contains instructions to:

- gain attention and stop automatic thoughts, e.g. *Stop Helen!*
- reduce arousal, e.g. *breathe out.*
- distract, e.g. *think of your green hill.*
- gain a sense of perspective and remember self-worth, e.g. *If this really needs to be dealt with I'll do it when I'm calm and clear headed!*
- a prompt to say *well done!* if successful (a tick or a thumbs-up!)

Some may like THE TRAFFIC LIGHT ROUTINE (see Appendix 4, page 233) but please note this could upset those who have been involved in a road traffic accident.

The idea is that reading the message or the card will interrupt the 'wind-up thoughts' and provide instruction on what to do:

Because when I am angry I can't think of anything else apart from how angry I am!

The coping card/book/message/picture should act as a firm instruction – 'The Bossy Book' – call it whatever is acceptable to the person concerned, make it a user-friendly gimmick!

Next week we shall make these visual prompts – cards, etc., so think of ideas of what to have on your 'coping card', and bring any pictures of scenes or calm hero figures, messages, poems, funny postcards, to the session.

Homework

Continue with the simple diaries.

Relaxation/arousal reduction

- Step 3 of OTSAR. Encourage each person to pace around remembering an angry situation, then to plonk themselves in a chair before starting the technique.
- Look at the anger thermometer and register the level of arousal before and after.

Therapist's notes

Feindler and Ecton (1986) describe how self-instruction has been used to train impulsive youngsters to provide themselves with internally generated verbal commands, or guiding statements. These help to inhibit an automatic aggressive response, and prompt a more adaptive one. They assert that 'adolescents who exhibit impulsive aggression have clear deficits in self-guiding speech'.

The original work on self-instruction was with impulsive 4-year-olds (Meichenbaum and Goodman 1971). It involved the therapist modelling a task whilst using first overt, and then covert, self-instruction to the child, who then repeated the process. This principle can be applied with individuals of any age if they require additional help in modelling and rehearsing the task.

SESSIONS 13/14

Welcome

Check homework and feedback

- Look at diaries.
- Use the thermometer to illustrate arousal levels described.

Recap

Last week:

- *we agreed that we all get unhelpful thoughts that can 'wind us up'*
- *we talked about how to interrupt or manage these by self-instruction*
- *we decided that prompt cards could be useful, either to look at or think of, when we feel ourselves boiling up.*

Practical Session

Making the coping cards, visual prompts, written or recorded scripts.

It is important that each person suggests what they would like as their prompt as this will be personal, unique and owned by the person concerned.

Discuss with each person:

- the choice of format
- what is acceptable to them (street cred)
- help them to decide on an instruction that they would take notice of if someone else gave it to them; e.g. *STOP GILL, breathe out and walk away.*

Because anger control is about self-management we are going to learn to instruct ourselves.

- Work in small groups and produce the visual or verbal prompts. It is a wise idea to make a copy of each person's instructions in case of their being lost, or laundered!)
- Re-introduce the idea of **role-play**. Therapists demonstrate how to use the instruction in a typically provocative situation, e.g.:

  Bill is sitting quietly in the lounge when along comes Fred looking for his lost cigarettes. Fred assumes that Bill must be sitting on them and tries to move Bill from the chair. Bill is annoyed and indignant, but manages to state that he is not sitting on them! Fred, however, is not interested in listening to any explanation, and an argument ensues.

- Repeat role-play but with Bill producing his card, or visualising it, and following the prompt shown:

STOP BILL – KEEP CALM – BREATHE AWAY THE ANGER!

- Discuss the difference in Bill's response and probable mood-matching from Fred as a result. Was there any difference in resulting behaviours? For example, did Fred apologise?
- Allow other members to 'have a go' and then discuss their efforts and feelings on how it went.

Discuss

- WHEN to use the instructions as a prompt.
- Re-cap on recognising the warning signs, otherwise learning when to use the coping skills will be difficult.
- By now it should be coming clear, to both the therapist and the participants, what are the likely triggers of anger.
- Various alternative scenarios can then be shown so as to demonstrate the use of the prompt.
- Explain that in time using these instructions will become a habit. So for example rather than producing the card each time anger is felt, it may be enough just to think of it, or tap it in the pocket.

Homework

1. Practise using the coping cards/instructions.
2. Continue to use diaries, if participants are still willing to do so. This helps to establish the particular patterns of anger, and also to monitor the severity and frequency (albeit from probably erratic recording) of the anger incidents.

Relaxation/arousal reduction

- Use step 3 of OTSAR – but perhaps include some self-statements to coincide with any coping cards/books.
- Look at the anger thermometer and register levels of arousal before and after.

Therapist's notes

If clients have self-monitoring or memory difficulties it may be necessary to encourage them to give licence to others to use discreet statements or gestures to cue them into using their personal coping routines. There may be some overlap with OTSAR scripts, see Appendix 1 for examples.

SESSIONS 15–18

Welcome

Feedback

- Look at diaries/bubbles or ask for oral feedback.

  - *Did anyone use their cards/books/instructions?*
  - *Were they useful?*

- If cards have been forgotten, lost or washed, be patient; it may take a while to establish the habit of using them. Some people do find it a strange thing to do, so encourage group members to support and prompt each other.

Note: If it is possible to pursue the cognitive restructuring work it will be necessary for the therapist to have some understanding of the important influence that cognitive therapy has had on work with anger problems.

The core of cognitive therapy is that our thoughts influence our mood, emotion, physical reaction and behaviour. So when teaching a client to manage their anger, the cognitive aspects are very important. The real challenge is helping clients to 'think themselves better' (see Therapist's notes overleaf).

Because of the difficulty that clients find with this abstract concept, therapists will no doubt have to tailor treatment delivery to their client group. Appendix 2 contains various exercises that have been devised to help explain that distorted cognitions set up individuals for anger.

It is expected that this stage may take a few sessions, say three or four, but, as already mentioned, if the therapist assesses that the client group cannot master the abstract concept continue to practise self-instruction training.

Therapist's notes

When a person is angry the thoughts that are flying through their head seem real, valid and justified, hence in turn they will maintain the anger arousal. On closer analysis the thoughts are often negative, distorted, perhaps unrealistic, and very unhelpful. Stallard (2002) refers to these as thinking errors, Burns (1990) refers to distorted or twisted thinking. Here are some examples of such thinking styles as applied to anger.

All-or-nothing thinking
You see things in black-or-white categories. Things are either right or wrong. If something is not as planned then it is a total failure. So if your benefit book has not yet arrived at the post office when you go to collect it, your thinking might be: *It's all gone totally wrong – it is a disaster!*

Overgeneralisation
You see a single event as part of a regular pattern. You make sweeping statements, often using the words 'always' and 'never', for example if the bus is late you might think: *That's it, it's* **always** *late, I'm* **never** *going on a bus again.*

Mental filter
You have selective attention to, or perception of, the situation, so important aspects are filtered out. This may lead you to discount the positives and pick on a single negative detail and dwell on it, which then winds you up. So when your friend comments on the really enjoyable meal that you had together, you would focus on *Oh but I spilt some of my drink! What a mess*, rather than taking a balanced view of the evening.

This is a common thinking style for people following disability, their attention being on what they now cannot do, rather than their achievements in rehabilitation. Such achievements are seen as a positive to the therapist but are taken as a given to the disabled person.

Jumping to conclusions (fortune telling)
You interpret things negatively even though there are no facts to support your conclusions. You guess what people are thinking (mind-reading) and then make up explanations for their behaviour; for example, one day you see your friend looking serious and rushing past, but because she does not speak to you, you think: *She hates me, so much for her friendship!*

(continued)

Therapist's notes (continued)

Magnification or catastrophising (making a mountain out of a molehill!)
You exaggerate the importance of your problem and feel it is a catastrophe; so, for example, if the washing machine is not emptying, your thinking might be: *How awful, how terrible, I've got no clothes to wear, I can't stand it, this is the end!*

Emotional reasoning
You take your emotion as evidence for the truth. So: *I feel angry; that proves that you must have been treating me badly.*

'Should' statements
'Shoulds, oughts and musts' are said to be illogical fixed rules! They are beliefs that are meant to motivate and set high standards. Yet instead they can be rigid demands and lead to guilt and disappointment when directed at yourself; or anger if directed at others. *I must never forget things, people should always be on time! Or we all ought to get equal amount of attention.* Clearly such fixed demands are unreasonable. Ellis, in Ellis and Tafrate (1997) calls these ***Musterbations;*** not surprisingly clients often seem to remember this term more readily than others, and as such it can be useful when helping them to identify their thinking styles or traps that they are setting for themselves.

These can be regarded as guidelines for operating in the world, or 'Rules for Life'. Some of these are absolute and fixed – *I should be able to cope;* and others are conditional – *unless I'm on my guard others will get one over on me.* (see more on page 191)

Labelling
You are quick to give yourself or others a negative label, attacking the person rather than what they did. This highly charged language leads to hostility and anger. So after one human mistake has been made, accusations of: *I'm useless!* or, *she's a lazy...., he's an excuse for a man!* might be said. Stallard (2002) calls these Dustbin labels.

Personalisation or blame (attributional bias)
You hold yourself or others responsible for some external event that is out of your/their control. **I** *got angry because* **you** *messed up everything today!*

Memorable illustrations of such limited thinking patterns can be seen in Stallard (2002).

By now, individuals will be developing a preferred routine of the arousal reduction. This may include some distraction, self-instruction or imagery.

- This session try out step 4 of OTSAR, the standing version.
- Look at the thermometer before and after.

SESSIONS 19–21

Welcome

Feedback

- Look at diaries/bubbles or ask for oral feedback.

  –Did anyone use their cards, scripts or instructions?
  –Were they useful?

- Again, be patient if cards have been forgotten or lost. Remember, it may take a while to establish the habit of using them. Some people do find it a strange thing to do, so encourage group members to support and prompt each other.

So far we have concentrated on reducing levels of anger arousal by learning ways to keep the body and thoughts calm. We also need to learn new ways of explaining ourselves effectively if the anger is justified and something has to be said. Therefore, during this part of the skill acquisition phase it is important to teach skill building, as well as arousal reduction, techniques.

Communication Skills

Effective communication skills can help us manage our anger by expressing our point assertively. However, being able to communicate what we feel and believe is a complex, interactive process that involves many cognitive processes, skills and behaviours (O'Neill 2002). We know that such skills are all less effective when anger arousal is high. Hence it is potentially an area where mistakes, mixed messages and frustration can occur.

Communication – Why it may go wrong	
Assessment of the situation	Extracting the social meaning using observation and listening skills, e.g reading facial expressions, body language, tone of voice and style.
Analysis of the Information	Speed of processing the information, taking the intended meaning and inference, filtering out any background noise, information overload.
Expressive language	Communication output involving both non-verbal (gestures, facial expression, distance) and verbal skills. May not monitor these and so know how they appear to others. May have word-finding and fluency problems; unable to formulate conversation, yet may easily produce automatic speech, particularly emotionally charged swear words (Van Lancker and Cummings 1999).
Past experiences	Memories are triggered (old tapes play) associated with previous situations and learned behaviours. May remember the feeling or affect more readily than what actually happened or was said; including any resolve.
Attitudes, expectations and beliefs	May have styles of thinking, very rigid rules, and beliefs that prime them for anger.
Self-worth and confidence	Telling self '*It's not worth your speaking up*', or a need to please '*Don't make a fuss, they won't like it*'. They may not have the expectation that assertion is an option for them.
Memory	Fear of forgetting may prompt impulsive or impatient responses.
Problem-solving skills	Choosing the time, place and person to communicate with.
Intense arousal such as anxiety or anger	Can affect all of these and reduce personal effectiveness.

The next few sessions will focus on the role of assertiveness and practising the skills. It is important to realise that although it may not feel like it, once we have the necessary skills we do then have a choice of how we respond when we feel 'fired up'. This choice can be talked about in principle (step 1) but carrying it out in vivo is more difficult (step 2) and requires practice, encouragement and gradual shaping of behaviours.

It may be necessary to teach the principles of assertion but scale it down to a prescriptive level that fits in with SIT, e.g. look down and breathe out, then look at the person and say *I'm feeling so stressed and tired, I need a minute to clear my head.*

Introduce the Assertive way

This shows three ways that we might behave when we feel 'fired up'. Let's look at each choice and decide which is best. Experience has shown that an effective way to demonstrate this point is for the therapist to role play in front of the group. Choose a situation (examples in Appendix 3, page 213) that is relevant to group members and work with the co-therapist.

Practical

Ask the group to watch and to notice:

- how you looked (non-verbal)
- what you said (checking interpretation and inference)
- what you did (behaviours and how they are rated, e.g. brave, wrong, deserve 'streetcred'.

  Use the Signpost Handout – *The Assertive Way* to introduce the terms passive, assertive and aggressive. (See Appendix 3 for handout (pages 216–217) and more on assertion training.)

What do these words actually mean?
Give short definitions:

Passive – Not saying what you need, want or believe in. Going along with others in order to be liked, or keep the peace, and then probably grumbling about it later. Feeling hurt, angry or used and walked over – like a doormat.

Assertive – Being assertive means saying clearly what we want, need and/or feel, whilst at the same time respecting the needs wishes and feelings of others.

Aggression – Being pushy and frequently overdoing it. Trying to force others into seeing your point and not listening to or considering their point of view. Threatening, intimidating, attacking and blaming, sarcastic, putting others down.

Brainstorm the costs and benefits of each style.

Did it pay off?
How would you feel afterwards – more or less angry? Guilty, powerful ....
Here are some example responses:

	Advantages – benefits	*Disadvantages – costs*
Passive	Don't upset others or make a fuss	Feel frustrated, and angry Problems don't get solved, needs don't get met People take advantage of you
Assertive	Proud of self! – I did OK! Respects self and others Respected by others More likely to get needs met Not a 'push-over' I said my piece People take me seriously Don't feel as angry	Others might be envious Might not always 'win' or get result looking for Could feel lonely if you are standing up to others
Aggressive	Showed 'em! Power? Opportunity to vent your feelings Felt great for a few minutes, then	Problems are not solved Lose respect BIG TIME Lose friends and family Problems may escalate Feel threatened and lonely Leaves you feeling guilty

So being assertive is a good way of responding when we feel 'fired up'.
Being assertive means:

- Taking responsibility for your own actions and choices.
- Being able to say NO if you want to.
- It is **not** about getting our own way or winning all the time.
- It is more about 'saying our piece' and consequently feeling that we have not let ourselves down.

- We do not have to be aggressive in order to get our point across!
- We do not have to be passive, have no control, and 'feel like a doormat'. This can mean that we get anxious, or that we then get annoyed with ourselves because we couldn't say what we felt. Sometimes that anger builds up, and we end up 'overdoing it' and being aggressive! Then we feel guilty.
- Being assertive is OK, it is NOT selfish and it often leads to a better end result!
- It is assertive to say if we don't understand – *could you please tell me again, I didn't catch it all.*
- Emphasise that when we have the necessary skills we do have a choice. Re-look at the **Signpost Handout – The Assertive Way.**

Let's learn how to be assertive (do this when you are calm)

Non-verbal behaviour. How do I look?

- Look the person in the eye.
- Stand tall and hold up your head.
- Have an open posture, no threats.
- Respect the other person's space, DO NOT stand too close.
- Use gestures that are firm but NOT threatening, e.g. open hands facing down when saying NO.
- Look as if you mean what you say, i.e. the non-verbal behaviour needs to match the words you are saying.

Verbal content. What to say (more examples in Appendix 3)

- Know what you want to say – plan it.
- Say it! Give a short simple message. *I feel worried about....*
- Stick to that message, repeat it if necessary.
- Speak firmly, don't whine!
- Be clear and calm.
- Use self-instruction, e.g. keep it clear, stick to the complaint, don't start criticising him/her.

Do not

- shout
- swear

- stare
- get too close or lean over
- use threatening or rude gestures, e.g. finger pointing or fists
- insist on your commands – try and be boss
- accuse or blame
- be sarcastic
- be over-apologetic or mumble.

Role-play

Role-play situations that are reported as causing anger arousal. Choose some where the end result was good, and some where despite the use of assertion, the end result was not the preferred one for the person concerned.
This reinforces the understanding that:

- Assertion is not just about getting what you want or winning, but about respectfully 'saying your piece'.
- It is necessary to choose the right time and place to use the skills.

As in Social Skills Training, follow the stages:

- dry run
- positive feedback (there is always something good you can say!)
- instruction and/or modelling using – assertion rather than aggression.
- include any coping cards, scripts or OTSAR; remember, keeping calm helps you to assert yourself more easily
- the practice stage, a re-run using the above or 'Take 2 of the movie'
- further feedback.

To shape behaviour and allow a sense of mastery, comment on:

- non-verbal behaviours
- voice tone
- listening skills
- what was said.

Remember, assertion is linked to confidence. We gain confidence from 'saying our piece' BUT we need confidence to say it, and the belief that we can and should say it!

Explore with the group why they think being assertive might be difficult. Hopefully this will elicit rules or beliefs such as:

I shouldn't speak up, it's rude
I'll only mess it up if I open my mouth
I must be loud and threatening to make people take notice of me

Any of these will discourage the person from using assertiveness. Although such beliefs may have been necessary during some chapters of the client's life, let's now re-evaluate. The worksheet in Appendix 4, page 240 aims to discover alternative beliefs/rules and behaviours which may be practised and tested out in order to gather evidence to disconfirm their unhelpful beliefs.

See also – The Rights Charter in Appendix 3, page 215

Homework

1. Practise using cards/scripts and arousal reduction when angry.
2. Try to get into the habit of checking levels of arousal by thinking of the thermometer.
3. Do this also each morning to start the day off well. If 'on the pink or red' use your breathing to calm down.
4. Say 'well done' to yourself when it works!
5. Keep a record of situations where you were assertive (see homework sheet in Appendix 3, page 218).

Relaxation/arousal reduction

- Step 4 of OTSAR, the standing version.
- Look at the thermometer before and after.

Therapist's notes

Use of video feedback.

There are many advantages to this, for it allows individuals to witness and evaluate their own behaviour before modifying it if necessary. Video can be a popular method of feedback, increasing the self-esteem and sense of participation. Yet be mindful of the individual's anxiety, for people do not learn well in a state of anxiety. When therapists participate in role-play it can be a source of amusement as well as a learning exercise for the group members. Also, use the video player to show excerpts from TV programmes (soaps) as examples of anger-provoking situations, and then discuss the response of the actors. This will help to clarify if clients are reading others' behaviour accurately.

REMEMBER: It is good practice to gain the client's permission before using video recording. Consult the local consent policy.

SESSIONS

Welcome

Review any angry situations arising from the diaries. Discuss alternative ways of handling situations and role-play.

Introduce – The Problem-Solving Routine

We often get angry if we come across what seems to be a problem to us. But remember:

- Problems are common.
- We can't avoid them.
- Many can be resolved.
- The problem-solving routine can help by taking the emotion out of the situation.
- Learn the routine when you are calm because when arousal levels are down, the memory and skill levels are up!
- When learning it, work in a group or with a therapist.
- Use the routine, don't be impulsive!

Here is a version that includes preliminary questions to prompt the angry person to:

a) inhibit their automatic response of anger and impulsivity and
b) take charge of their arousal before deciding if there is a problem to solve.

This is a structured routine that guides the person to actively generate a solution. The process looks lengthy but with practice individuals learn to weigh up the pros and cons more quickly.

The Problem-solving worksheet containing fewer instructions than this session prompt sheet is in Appendix 3, page 219. It therefore offers more writing space and is less visually stimulating.

Therapist's notes

A great deal has been written about the problem-solving approach based on the work of D'Zurilla and Goldfried (1971) and it has been used successfully with children, adolescents and adults. It consists of 6 basic steps:

1) Identify the problem
2) Think of all possible solutions
3) Consider the consequences of each option. Include positive and negative, short and long term, i.e. feel better for two minutes, but get into trouble big time in the long term!
4) Pick the best option
5) Do it
6) Evaluate

To most of us, this process is so routine that we are unaware of the cognitive operations that we follow. However, in many instances, clients' cognitive deficits cause them to have difficulty in any one, or more, of those stages. Therefore, learning the problem-solving routine is an important component of the skill acquisition phase of anger management.

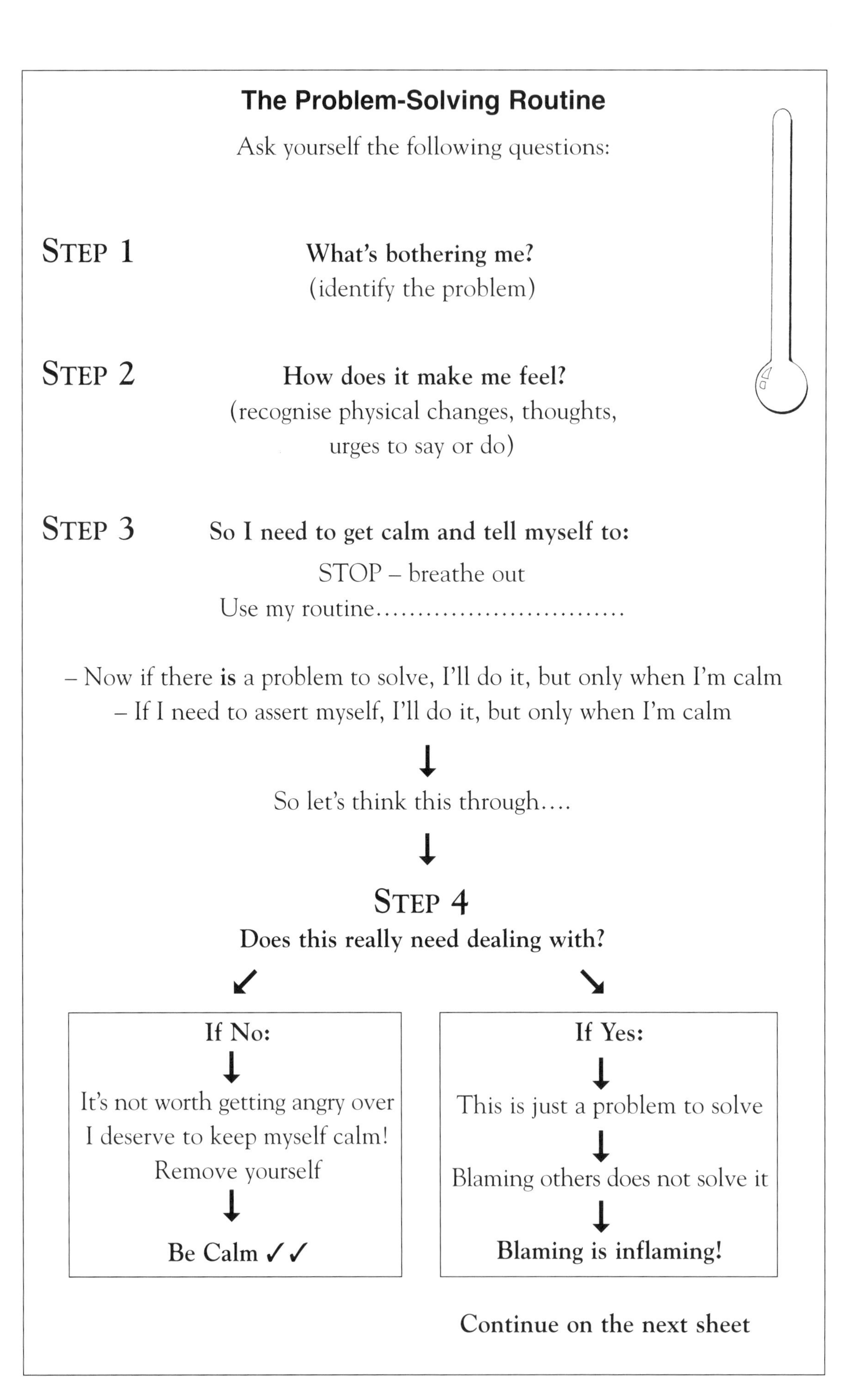

The Problem-Solving Routine

Ask yourself the following questions:

STEP 1 **What's bothering me?**
(identify the problem)

STEP 2 **How does it make me feel?**
(recognise physical changes, thoughts, urges to say or do)

STEP 3 **So I need to get calm and tell myself to:**
STOP – breathe out
Use my routine.............................

– Now if there **is** a problem to solve, I'll do it, but only when I'm calm
– If I need to assert myself, I'll do it, but only when I'm calm

↓

So let's think this through....

↓

STEP 4
Does this really need dealing with?

↙ ↘

If No:
↓
It's not worth getting angry over
I deserve to keep myself calm!
Remove yourself
↓
Be Calm ✓✓

If Yes:
↓
This is just a problem to solve
↓
Blaming others does not solve it
↓
Blaming is inflaming!

Continue on the next sheet

STEP 5 **What do I want to happen?**
(select a realistic goal)

STEP 6 **What can I do?**
(think of a few alternatives)

A	B	C

STEP 7 **Consider consequences of each one**
(positive and negative, short and long term)

A	B	C
+	+	+
–	–	–

STEP 8 **What is my decision? –**
circle the best option above

STEP 9 **Plan how to carry this out**

STEP 10 **Now do it!** (implementation)

STEP 11 **How did it work?**
(evaluate, was it successful? Would you do it again? If not, would your second choice have worked?)

Practical

- Decide on some problem situations, set the scene, and practise using the routine.
- It is advisable to learn the routine when in a calm state.
- Try and elicit thoughts and ideas that clients might have when they are in such situations and feeling angry. Suggestions may reflect impulsive and dysfunctional ideas. Point out that we are more likely to censure the 'daft' ideas when we are calm because when the anger is down, the judgement is up! (see cartoon (below) and Appendix 1). Discuss the disadvantages of both the idea and the arousal.
- Now it will be clear why the routine begins with a prompt to self-monitor, followed by self-instruction such as: *OK it's not a total mess, it's just a problem to solve.*

Homework

- Practise using the problem-solving routine, it might be a good idea to get someone else to do it with you until you are familiar with it.
- As always, begin the practice with problems that are reasonably easy to solve, not an insurmountable one!

Relaxation/arousal reduction

Continue practising whichever method is popular.

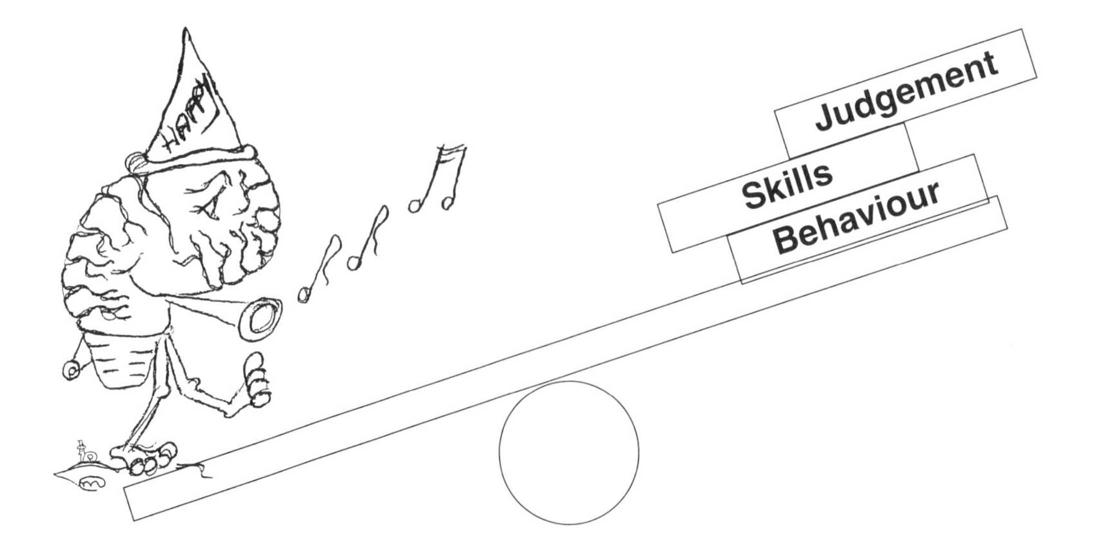

SESSIONS 25–28

Welcome

Feedback

- From the week – look at diaries/bubble pictures or ask for oral feedback.
- Discover incidents that were handled well (remained in control) as well as those that were a problem.

Role-play

- Role-play any scenarios that presented difficulties. Do a dry run, feedback, consider alternative responses, re-run, etc.

Recap

In earlier sessions:

- We have talked about wind-up thoughts and more helpful thoughts.
- Some of these are on your coping cards.
- So far we have used the cards and routines when we start to feel angry, but they can also be used at other times.

How to prepare for a potentially provoking situation

Often provocation occurs with very little warning but at other times we know that a potentially provoking situation is looming.

Refer to the list made in session 3 and brainstorm additional ideas of other situations, such as:

- Mental Health Review Tribunal
- meeting with an important official
- having to spend time with someone that you do not like
- watching a football match on TV with someone who supports the other team!

Some of these situations are VERY PROVOKING and others less so. Try to establish a hierarchy of provocations because when we practise preparing for the situations we shall start with the less provoking and work up to the VERY PROVOKING! Such situations can be prepared by using the:

Stress Inoculation Training – SIT

The principle is to train the individual to use self-instruction statements when approaching, confronting or leaving an angry situation. This should enable them to deal with that situation calmly. It works by encouraging:

a) Direct arousal reduction – *my muscles are getting tight – time to relax.*
b) Indirect arousal reduction through interrupting and challenging the thoughts *STOP – don't allow yourself to go up the thermometer, check the facts!*

See Appendix 2 for extra ideas of self-statements. The complexity of this technique can be graded, an example of a simplified, repetitive self-statement to reduce arousal and increase the feeling of control is demonstrated below.
In the exercise below the phrase '**get calm**' will be used as a prompt to carry out the quick 'on-the-spot' arousal reduction, or OTSAR, that we have been practising each week. Naturally, the wording can be adjusted to suit individuals' taste and choice, try to ensure that it does not conflict with the message on the coping card/script.

Check

Make sure that everyone understands what is meant by **get calm**, practise when sitting, standing, queuing ...

NOW APPLY THIS TO A SITUATION – such as one of those suggested in the brainstorming exercise. Write a list of prompts on the board.

1. Prepare and reassure yourself before the situation – *Remember what you're trying to sort out and stick to that.*
2. **Get calm** (deep breath, self-instruction).
3. Imagine how it might be. (They may lead to increased anger arousal.)
4. **Get calm**.

5. Think of the key points that you want to say – take responsibility if you are in the wrong.
6. **Get calm.**
7. Imagine what the other person is likely to say – and listen!
8. **Get calm.**
9. Say your piece – key points, then listen, don't argue back.
10. **Get calm.**
11. Resolve or accept the situation, it is not about winning, but it's about being assertive and feeling good with yourself, because at least you did your best!
12. *Well done! I can only do my best.*

Suggest that the client 'runs through' the procedure in their mind (or talks it through with the therapist) before they actually practise it.

TRY THE TECHNIQUE OUT ON A SITUATION THAT IS ONLY A LITTLE PROVOKING and therefore has a good chance of success. Later on you can try it out in a more provoking situation, and so on.

Afterwards, congratulate yourself!

Homework

Practise using the new technique when there is a situation that is known to be potentially arousing.

Relaxation/arousal reduction

Step 4 of OTSAR – standing version.

Therapist's notes

It is hoped that by now individuals should have acquired some of the skills necessary to help them manage their anger. However, therapists should not assume that skills learned will generalise to the 'real world'. Imagery and behavioural rehearsal, role-play, modelling and graduated *in vivo* practice, all contribute to generalisation.

SESSIONS 29–30

COPING WITH SETBACKS

Welcome

Feedback

- *How's the week been?*
- *Did anyone need to use the problem-solving routine?*

Look at examples of situations (from diaries or feedback) when anger was:

- handled well and the individual kept control – encourage them to give themselves a pat on the back, they were in charge!
- anger arousal was up, and things did not end up so well.

Look what happened in problem scenarios, draw attention to the cost of what happened, e.g.:

- observations increased as behaviour was thought to be risky
- feeling upset
- brooding (ruminating)
- losing friends.

Now prompt the individual to ask the question, *did my anger help me in the situation?* and if their answer is *NO – then let's look again at what happened.*

So you had a 'blip', a crisis, a rage – discover their word and use it.

- Reinforce any motivation to change but suggest that there is a chance that these 'blips' may occasionally still happen. This does not mean that you are condoning them, but that you are realistically acknowledging human fallibility.

To learn what we can from this let's use the worksheet found on page 238 in Appendix 4.

- Identify any positives and also things still to work on.
- Discuss alternative ways of reacting and have a re-run of the situation.
- The trick is to learn to spot the high-risk situations and plan for them; or involve someone you trust and ask for help or advice

Might you ever need a back-up plan if and when there is a 'blip' ....?

- Suggest it might be a good idea to have an agreed routine that others might be aware of.
- *Who will you talk to?* What key statement or sign can you give them to ensure they appreciate that you really need them?
- *Where is a safe place to go to cool down?*

Homework

Practise the range of skills learned. Offer suggestions as to the type of situations to tackle, thereby helping the client to grade the application of skill and assisting them not inadvertently to set themselves up to fail!

Relaxation/arousal reduction

Continue practising whichever method is popular.

Therapist's notes addressing all aspects of the anger

What we **do** when we are angry is very important, particularly to those other people around us! If we are able to walk away from a situation without getting into a row, that is an adaptive way of coping. But is it a complete answer? The person who is walking away with a high level of physiological arousal and racing wind-up thoughts would probably say no!

So beware, the behaviour is only part of it. What about the level of arousal that the person is still left with? If it is not dealt with, the potential for another flare-up of anger is a strong possibility. This may even follow a slight irritation and result in what seems a disproportionate amount of anger. Arousal that is prolonged by rumination can transfer to subsequent situations of provocation. Zillman (1983) described this process as 'excitation transfer'.

So it is important to tackle all three components of the anger. The physiological arousal must be reduced as well the cognitions challenged and reappraised. Put in context, this means that removing yourself from a potentially angry situation is good.

BUT REMEMBER OTSAR!

ADDITIONAL SESSIONS (OPTIONAL EXTRAS)

ADDITIONAL SESSION 1

HOW TO COPE WITH BEING TOLD NO!

Discuss

- Does this happen to everyone at some time or another?
- It is just a part of life?
- Might there be a valid reason for the NO?
- Suggest some common situations.

Do we like to be told NO?
What is the effect on us?

Situations

You have a request, and despite an assertive explanation, reasoning, etc. the answer is NO!

Examples:

- a trip to town
- a home visit
- you need some of your money out of the safe but staff are busy and can't listen; he/she indicates *come back later*
- you want to speak to your case manager, or social worker, but you are told that he/she is busy all day.

What to do

Take notice of the warning signs.

Self-monitor any change in:

- body arousal (up the thermometer)
- thoughts (wind-up thoughts)
- voice getting louder.

Take action

- Use self-instruction – remember your card if you have one.
- Interrupt your thoughts – *Stop Helen.*
- Breathe away the anger – take two deep breaths.
- Walk away from the situation.
- Then use calming thoughts:

  Oh well, let's hope I can go next week.
  Yes this is annoying, but I will cope.
  Maybe it's not their fault.

- Use distraction that demands concentration, e.g. count backwards from 100 or 10.
- Look at a picture on your card.
- Imagine your peaceful spot, i.e. that scene of a hill in Ireland!

Role-play

- A situation that has caused a group member difficulty in the past.

Include OTSAR, self-instruction or thinking of the coping card/script before following the instructions.

Praise if it works!

ADDITIONAL SESSION 2

DEALING WITH TEASING AND PROVOCATION

Discuss

Why people tease:

- *Is it to get a response or to get others into trouble?*
- *Do you ever tease others?*
- *How do you feel when you are teased?*

Brainstorm

How does being teased affect your:

- thoughts (cognition)
- feelings (arousal)
- behaviour (What do you do? Do you ever react?).

What are the consequences of your behaviour?

What to do

Take notice of the warning signs

Self-monitor any

- wind-up thoughts
- body tension, etc.

Take action

- Use self-instruction and card if used.

- Interrupt and challenge your thoughts, – STOP HELEN, THINK THIS THROUGH.
- Breathe away the anger, take two deep breaths.

This is to 'KEEP A LID ON' your arousal whilst you consider the best way to react. Try to think of a way that will not allow the situation to blow up, yet not leave you feeling that the other person has got the better of you.

Choices

Use problem-solving methods to decide which of the following to use:

- Ignore the person – remember people tease to get results; if you give a response, they have won! Don't provoke or tease in return.
- Leave, walk away.
- Make a joke!
- Agree with the teasing.
- Imagine them wearing a funny hat or silly costume.

KEEP COOL AND BE PLEASED WITH YOURSELF!

Some of these are not easy to do, but tell yourself that *It will be worth it* and remember, if you don't react badly you will have got the better of them!

Role-play

- Situations that were mentioned in the discussion at the beginning of the session.
- Use the problem-solving process to make a choice of which course of action to take.

Praise if it works !

Therapist's notes

A visual flow chart illustrating choices is included in Appendix 4. This can offer structure to the decision-making process, see page 239.

ADDITIONAL SESSION 3

COPING WITH CRITICISM

Discuss

- Why we might be criticised?
- *Has anyone been criticised recently?*
- Make a list of examples.

Brainstorm

How does being criticised affect your:

- thoughts
- feelings
- behaviour – how do you react?

Do a cost/benefit analysis for each reported behaviour and then divide the behaviours into those that seem to make matters worse and do not pay-off, versus more appropriate responses. For example:

	OR	
– argue back		– speak politely
– swear		– don't swear
– run off		– stay and listen
– aggressive tone		– assertive tone
– ignore and look away showing no interest at all		– listen to the other person's point of view then they may listen to yours
– rude non-verbal signs		– no rude gesture
– sarcasm		– no clever comments
– laugh at the other person		– listen to their point

There may be a difference in your reaction depending upon whether the criticism is justified or not, i.e. fair or unfair.

What to do

Either way,

- Listen, and check that you understand what was said.
- Look at the other person.
- Remember the thermometer, monitor levels.
- Use self-instruction and arousal reduction.
- Congratulate yourself if you stay cool!
- Take time to decide if the criticism is justified or not.

If justified

- Agree, admit to your mistakes (be assertive). *Yes you're right I was slapdash.*
- Explain your reason if you wish (but NOT lengthy excuses).
- Apologise if necessary.

If unjustified

- Politely, but firmly disagree – *No I don't agree that I was lazy…*
- Give an explanation; if there is another reason – *I was resting, I know I need to pace myself.*
- Ask what makes them think that.
- Express how you felt – upset, etc.

Practical

To role-play either giving or receiving criticism can be awkward for both parties. Therefore, it is advisable to ease into this technique by first using other exercises such as:

- A discussion when people have opposing views on cars, smoking, football teams, music, etc. Allow participants to participate in this, or watch a pre-recorded video of people doing this. Here, criticism is aimed at the person's views rather than at the person themselves. Discuss the necessity to respect others' views and the importance of not taking things personally.

- watching a pre-recorded video of staff being criticised, use examples when good and poor responses are shown, then discuss.
- As individuals watch the recording and observe the scene without being on the receiving end of the anger, it may be easier for them to make an objective observation. Encourage them to use their problem-solving skills to encourage a rational choice about the response taken.

Role-play

Role-play situations that were mentioned at the beginning of the session, e.g.:

- You're late.
- You're untidy.
- Your work is not good enough.
- Your flat/house is untidy and the care worker has just been to visit and suggests you clean it up!
- You're useless.

The empty chair technique can be used if people initially find it difficult or confusing to criticise other group members during role-play.

Therapist's Notes

As stated on page 115 people are often quick to label others. When this happens any criticism of a person's performance or behaviour becomes aimed at the person as a whole, e.g. 'You're completely useless', rather than 'you didn't do that job very well'. Being criticised as a person feels worse and like a general attack rather than a specific explanation of what they did not like.

ADDITIONAL SESSION 4

BEING ON THE RECEIVING END OF ANGER

Discuss

- What this might mean.
- It could be someone 'sounding off' about others or feeling angry with you.
- *Have we all been in this position?*

Brainstorm

How did this affect our:

- thoughts?
- feelings?
- behaviour?

A person on the receiving end of anger, or just witnessing the behaviour of an angry person, can experience a great range of 'hot cognitions'. These will depend upon that person's 'old tapes' (past experiences, memories and expectations) and on whom the target of the anger is directed. It is common for individuals to experience fear, a need for revenge, worry or insecurity and, in turn, they may respond with attack, defence or avoidance. Anyone with a history of abuse may readily perceive the anger to be directed at them, even if it is not.

Being close to someone who is highly aroused and angry can be unsettling.

Anger can be infectious!

Do we have a choice whether we accept the anger?

Try and step out of the situation and ask yourself:

- what is the problem?
- what choices do I have?

Look at the costs and the benefits of each of the behavioural responses that individuals suggest, e.g.:

Be angry and verbally aggressive in response
Quietly take it all in
Run off and hit something

What were the consequences? Did they make the situation better or worse?

What to do

- Listen and try to understand what the person is actually angry about.
- Remember you will not listen properly unless you stay calm.
- Give the angry person space.
- Breathe slowly.
- It might help to imagine yourself out of the situation, say watching it on TV.
- Think clearly: what actually is the problem?
- Remain calm – tone of voice.
- No sudden movements or large gestures (these can be perceived as threatening).
- Use self-statements to keep yourself calm.

For example:

Sometimes I've been this angry, it will pass.
He/she must really be unhappy to be acting like this.
I'm not going to let him/her get to me.
I'll get out now and talk to him/her later.
It's a real shame he/she's that upset.
Don't discuss it like this, we'll both say things we don't mean.

- Try to see it from their point of view before you decide if you agree or disagree with their annoyance.

- When you are both more calm and ready to talk, sit down and continue as above.
- Don't take all that is said personally, but if you made a mistake, be brave enough to admit it!
- Apologise if you are at fault.
- This does not mean that you always do everything wrong!
- Ask if there is anything you can do to make the person feel better.

Role-play

Role-play situations that were mentioned in the initial discussion (the therapist may have to take the role of the angry person). Discuss the result, feeling of control and the use of self-statements.

ADDITIONAL SESSION 5

CARRYING A GRUDGE

Discuss

- What we mean by this.
- *Have we ever done it?*
- *Is it worse with certain people?*
- *Does it last for a long time?*
- *Do we remember grudges more easily than good experiences with the person?*
- *Do we file those in the dustbin?*

Situations

For example:

- You have been upset by another client spreading rumours about you, teasing, or name calling, but you have to live in the same hostel/ward as them!
- Your neighbour told the warden that you had broken the rules by entertaining people of the opposite sex after hours.
- You have been lied to or let down.

Brainstorm

- *What will happen when you see that person?*
- *Will your level of arousal change (go up on the thermometer)?*
- *Will there be any warning signs?*

  such as changes to your:
  - body
  - thoughts
  - behaviour.

What do you do?

- get revenge?
- throw something?
- take it out on someone else?
- self-harm?
- or what?

Do a cost/benefit analysis for each suggestion.

REMEMBER:	**We can decide not to allow other people to hurt us.** Yes, but if we forgive them and let it pass, it may feel as if we are letting ourselves down; **BUT** Consider the bad effects on us if we don't . . . . ? We don't have to like them, but we do need to be able to live happily with ourselves!

So what are the alternatives?

It depends if you feel you must assert your feelings about the grudge. If so:

- Be firm but CALM when you tell the other person that you do not like what they are doing, and please will they stop it. Such assertion can give a sense of power and increased self-esteem.
- But remember that there is a chance you could risk escalating the arousal of the other person!

Or if you are able to keep a low profile and not let the comments get to you:

- Why should you let that person wind you up?
- You deserve better!
- Do your OTSAR!

However, when circumstances force you to be together:

Remember

Use self-statements to prompt the use of:

- arousal reduction
- your card if you have one.

Do this

- when you know you will be seeing them
- whilst you are in their company
- to reduce your arousal if it starts to increase
- when you have managed not to BLOW-IT!
- congratulate yourself if the end result is better than usual.

Role-play

Role-play situations such as:

- being shut in a lift with another person with whom you always row
- trying to watch the TV when people are nattering and bothering you
- being pestered by another client for cigarettes, money, etc.
- having to work alongside ‘that person’ who now goes out with your girl/boyfriend.

RECAP SESSIONS

Welcome/feedback

These sessions aim to recap what has been learnt over the past weeks.

Key points

Recognising the signs of anger: *What are they?* Brainstorm:

- signs of physiological arousal
- changes in cognition
- behavioural changes.

What do we do when we feel the warning signs?

Give each person an opportunity to reuse the worksheet 'Ways To Calm' (Appendix 4, page 236). Give them a different colour pen and suggest that they add what they now do when they are beginning to feel angry and how they cope. Compare the suggestions offered when the worksheet was used before (session 10). Summarise key points, i.e.:

- take action, take charge of the anger – see worksheet in Appendix 4, page 241
- use the coping card/book
- long slow outward breath followed by two complete deep breaths
- count backwards, etc.

Once the instinctive response is arrested, leave it for the moment, calm down and decide what to do next, e.g.:

- Let it drop – maybe there is another side to it.
- Be assertive – if a point has to be made.
- Solve the problem (with help?).

- Think it through with someone, maybe have a quick grumble, but then try to see it from all sides.
- Humour!

Whichever method you use, if it works be pleased that you felt calm and 'kept a lid on' your anger! . . . . WELL DONE!

Remember other ways of preventing anxiety, stress and anger

Explain the importance of preventing stress and anger by adjusting lifestyle and habits and the importance of leisure activities, e.g.:

- purposeful use of time leading to satisfaction with our own efforts
- setting some time aside each day to do something enjoyable (your quality time)
- niggles and frustrations do not seem so bad if balanced with pleasurable activities. Plan a regular relaxing treat.
- self-esteem and mood are very closely linked to anger
- sleeping regularly
- eating a balanced diet
- avoiding alcohol and drugs
- getting some fresh air every day
- explaining your worries to a trusted person, and asking for help if needed.

Therapist's notes

Learning to manage our anger is a complex task involving many components. Consequently this manual has touched on a number of training techniques, some of which will be more useful than others to any one person. It is hoped that the client has now built up a picture of his/her patterns of anger and of his/her preferred ways of coping. It is likely that in the past they will have been given conflicting advice of what to **do** when they are angry, rather than developing an understanding of, and then devising customised ways of coping with, their anger.

Finish

Allow time for each client to share their discoveries and new routines in particular. Encourage participants to help and remind each other to use their new skills to manage their anger. Encourage mutual support for all.

BRINGING THE TECHNIQUES OUT OF THE TREATMENT ROOM

We cannot just deliver the treatment and hope that generalisation of skills will happen naturally and that behaviour acquired in the therapy session will carry over to other situations. Plans have to be made to ensure the transfer of skills, including tailoring the process to suit the needs of the individual.

Throughout the course we have been mindful of individual needs, and of the role of environmental triggers in the client's world. Both of these factors can affect the success of generalisation of skills.

So as to increase the likelihood of clients respecting their vulnerabilities, and practising effective skills, assist them to create a summary of the key points that they have discovered and need to remember. Consider which type of personalised package will be most helpful to your clients.

A personal Action Plan

Describing the key points of the person's anger arousal and their plan of how to manage it. This can include their own visual reminders or any memorable prompts. See worksheet on page 153.

For other clients it may be therapeutic to assist them to create a fuller:

Individualised summary

Often called a blueprint in cognitive therapy, which explains their triggers, patterns of anger and ways of coping, see examples on pages 154 and 156.

The purpose of this is to:

a) Re-affirm their newly acquired skills.

b) Have a written record for the benefit of the client and others involved in their care. This may include any prompts or cues that the client has given others licence to use.

c) The client may like to give the pack an idiosyncratic title such as 'My flapping pack', 'This is me', or 'The how I tick book'. See an example on page 154.

Some of the key points can be implemented in the recap sessions, for example:

- Overlearning a particularly difficult skill such as ignoring baiting from others – practise and praise success heartily!
- Fading of prompts from others or from self. By this stage many clients find that they do not need to get their coping card out and look at it; instead, a gentle tap of their pocket will act as a reassuring prompt.
- Self-reinforcement, or planning a regular treat for yourself if there has been a trouble-free period. Decide how this is to be evaluated and by whom, i.e. will it be up to the client to record or will they be dependent

upon feedback from others? Ensure that the goals are achievable and that the frequency of the treats is such that they are worth working for!

- Expecting that when clients try out new skills outside the treatment room the response of others cannot be guaranteed. At the end of treatment it is advisable to role-play what the client can self-instruct if the person on the receiving end is discouraging, or even irrational!

Other methods to assist generalisation of skills

In vivo practice for homework

- Set clear goals to achieve (small achievable realistic steps).
- Think it through before actually attempting the step.
- Prepare a coping routine that is usable by the person, i.e. self-instructions, arousal reduction techniques, distraction.
- How to remember it? reminders, prompt cards, tapes, etc.
- Rehearse using imagery or role-play.
- Self-monitor before completing the task.
- Now put into practice.
- Ensure arousal is DOWN before leaving the situation.
- Evaluate:
  - reward the positives
  - shape behaviour
  - be encouraging!

Follow-up sessions

Follow-up sessions, delivered on a less regular basis than the main course of treatment, have been shown to be a productive way of retaining some support, yet withdrawing structure and prompts. Fading the frequency of the sessions avoids a sudden ending of the treatment and clients are not able to join the '*been there, done that – now I can forget it*' frame of mind!

Follow-up sessions act as a 'top up' or booster for all the hard work that has been carried out. Clients can be given reinforcement for the times that they coped well with their anger, and learn further about difficulties they may have encountered. Any unforeseen problems that may have occurred can be examined, coping styles identified and their implementation prepared for.

The importance of data collection, from whichever source is practical, completes the monitoring of progress (see page 59).

Name ________________________________ **Date** __________

Personal Action Plan

At times I get angry; these times are usually when

....

....

....

....

I know I'm angry because I can recognise that:

I am **T**hinking

....

My body is **F**eeling

....

I am **D**oing the following things

....

The reasons I would like to change are:

....

So I will try to interrupt or arrest the anger if I:

1) **T**hink or say this to myself

....

2) **D**o a calming breath OUT

Then check how my body is feeling, has the thermometer stopped rising? If no, then do more slow breathing

Now, if there is something to deal with or a problem to solve,
I will do it calmly when I have:
Planned it
Prepared what to say or do
Practised it then it is more likely to be **P**urrrrrrfect!

SUMMARY OF MY MANAGING ANGER WORK

Example of an individual summary of work with a client who has learning disabilities

Name: *Fred*

My anger can cause me a lot of trouble and grief because:

sometimes I hit others, have lost friends, am not allowed out on my own, I don't like to feel out of control.

The warning signs are:

a sudden rush of strength in my body, heart beats faster, fists clench, I stare at the other person, nasty thoughts.

I know that on some days I am not as tolerant if:

I'm hot, tired, had bad thoughts in the night, or have been worrying.

My anger triggers are:

- *people looking at me (I can think they are a threat)*
- *people not understanding me*
- *getting blamed*
- *people speaking very fast*
- *being made fun of*
- *I often 'get the wrong end of the stick'.*

I have learned the following techniques to use each day:

- *regularly monitor how I feel*
- *try to start off the day calm*
- *use my coping book when I start to feel angry*

If I monitor that I'm over 30 on the thermometer, I need to take action
And use

– *breathing techniques* – ***breathe OUT first then '3 in and 4 out'***
– *tell myself quieten down and cool it*
– *leave, think it through, and decide if*
a) I need to say something when I'm calm or
b) it's not worth a disagreement.

Have a regular 'Chill Out' time each day.

- Remind myself that it is NOT weak or cowardly to walk away from an annoying situation, it is just good sense!

My danger zone starts at number .... 60........
I must use my coping skills before I get near to that number (30+).

If I can't manage to take charge of my anger I need to:

Tell my carer (give him the quick signal, my T= time out sign), then go off and have a quick run/fast walk, then slow down and focus on my coping book

Well done!

MY FLAPPING PACK

Example of part of a blueprint completed during treatment with an out patient who has had a brain injury

What have I learned?

My anger was a real problem for both me and my family. The sessions have helped me develop understanding that:

Anger and anxiety affect our thoughts, body arousal and what we do, e.g.:

THINK → FEEL → DO

My goal was to manage my temper and learn some self-management skills.

The warning signs for me are

- my breathing gets faster and heart goes bang, bang
- sweating
- feeling sick and churning stomach
- headache
- sometimes I cry
- dry mouth
- hands are clenched and ready to punch
- others say my facial expression always gives away how I'm feeling – my eyes narrow and I frown
- my voice gets louder and I swear a lot.

Triggers for me

- Tiredness and fatigue, mornings particularly bad!
- A bad head – too long on the computer or TV makes this worse.
- Not drinking enough liquid or eating properly leads to my being crabby.
- Not being able to find what I want to say = frustrating and I feel stupid.
- Sudden, frightening noises particularly at night. I always think the worst and feel anxious. Then I get annoyed about why there has been a noise and the anxiety changes into anger.
- If I forget to take my carbamazapine I feel more impatient and 'sparky'. I'm also annoyed with myself for not taking it!
- Coping with change as I can't instantly think through the situation.
- Expectations of myself and others – I can be hard on myself, and quick to think that others are being 'shirty with me'.
- My 'rules for life' that set me up for frustration, anger, disappointment and self-righteousness, e.g.:

  *People **should always** do things properly*
  *They are **never** happy with me*

- Things happening that press my Ouch Buttons! E.g. *People testing me or asking me things, which makes me feel a failure. Once I feel like a failure I'm looking out for more examples of my failings. Then I get all fired up.*

So how do I recognise the warning signs?

- By regularly self-monitoring – think of my scale.
- Keep the thermometer and recording sheet on the fridge door (until the monitoring becomes second nature to me).
- If I'm above 30 – Take action!
- Do my calming breaths and think it through.

IT IS IMPORTANT TO REMEMBER

My anger and anxiety can be made worse by a low opinion of myself. Therefore I need to try to make sure that I am not exposing myself to situations that actually keep proving my point.

So Planning is really important for me. I need to:

Set realistic expectations and targets for myself. Keep them small, achieve them and be pleased with myself! It might be an idea to keep a record of these achievements, so that I can check on my progress in future.

Zoe, don't be too hard on yourself!

✓ For example, it is unrealistic to expect me to be able to effectively receive or absorb information when I'm tired, wound-up, or if there is a lot of noise around. Therefore, the way information is delivered is important. It's also OK for me to say if I didn't quite understand things.

✓ When I go on the computer I need to set the pinger in the other room so that it will interrupt me and then I will have to break off to switch it off.

✓ I need to make sure that 'I'm on the blue' and it is reasonably quiet before I make decisions or arrangements.

✓ Sometimes if I'm too tired, or worried my sleep pattern can get disturbed. Then it is important not to sleep too long in the day even if I'm tired, or I will not get it right again.

✓ Schedule in some 'peace times' each day, such as sitting quietly on your own.

Because, if I practise keeping calm, I can rise above annoyances, frustrations and other silly ....!

I deserve that!

But if I do have a 'bad day' . . . .

What is useful for me to do when I'm trying to cope?

✓ Self-monitor – think of the thermometer! – how much tension/ anger?

✓ Give myself time-out of the situation – don't try and sort it out there and then. Go for a walk or 'a chill'.

✓ Get my body calm –

use breathing techniques,
my relaxation tape or
imagine floating gently in the
balloon . . . .

Over the hill with the cool air on your face,
your body feels light as you land safely
on a bed of straw

– this calms me even if it scares Helen silly!

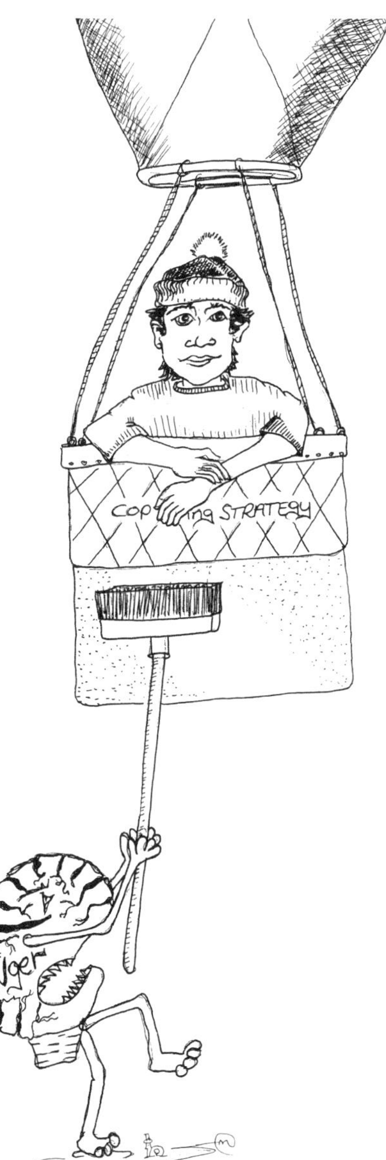

✓ Self instruction (or talking to myself!) to stop the 'wind-up thoughts' or NATS and then think 'Is there another way of looking at this?'

✓ Remember to respect others' ways, just as I like others to respect me.

When people do things differently to the way I might, it annoys me. This is because I don't understand where they are coming from, whereas 'my way' would have been more simple (at least to me!).

When this happens – **I need to think:**

STOP and then tell myself

That's just their way, it's different to my way, but it does not mean it's wrong. I have to respect we are different.

If you really do feel you have to say something to assert yourself, suggest you both talk about how to solve 'the problem'. Make sure you are calm first!

If I'm above 30 on my scale DON'T speak!

– Zippy Zoe!!

Zoe – don't go there!

APPENDIX

APPENDIX 1

THE PHYSIOLOGICAL COMPONENT

RELAXATION AND AROUSAL REDUCTION

Increased physiological activity and muscular tension are often early signs of anger arousal. They usually occur before any behavioural action is taken. In the early stages of anger management treatment individuals may not be aware of these physiological warning signs. Therefore, it is necessary that they have education about the benefits of relaxation and an opportunity to develop awareness of tension areas. Only then can the individual learn to induce a relaxation response which is a crucial part of managing anger. As we said on page 3, emotional arousal also has a detrimental effect on a person's cognitive function.

The benefits of keeping calm

Can listen properly (pay attention) = **Perform better, I deserve that!**
Concentrate
Problem solve
Question and reason
Make reasonable choices
Think what to say
Find words more easily
Can use strategies or tricks to keep calm
Body and general health like it
e.g. blood pressure is low
Sleep better

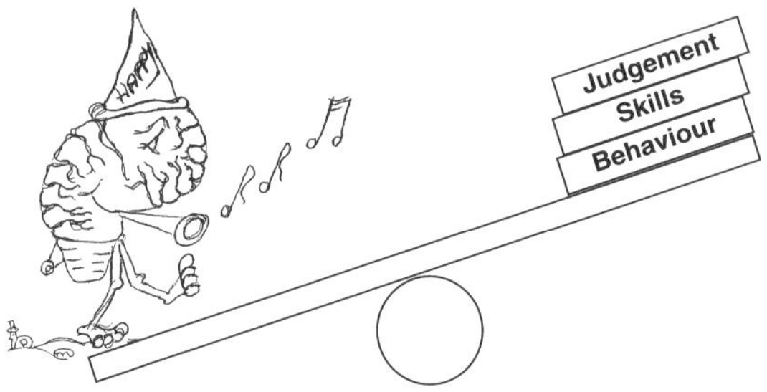

If the physiological arousal can be arrested or reduced this should, in turn, reduce the likelihood of any impulsive and problematic behaviour being triggered. Being able to 'calm down' on cue happens only after a great deal of dedicated training and practice. Yet this is what we are aiming for in managing anger. Some clients may already be familiar with, and practising, the techniques on a regular basis; this of course will be a great advantage to them. Yet many clients are resistant to relaxation for a variety of reasons because they:

- have tried it unsuccessfully
- can't see its relevance to managing anger, it is too passive to use in those heated moments
- have not been able to appreciate the difference between tense and relaxed
- hate lying down, feel vulnerable with their eyes closed
- have time to ruminate, which in turn increases arousal
- relaxation; it's for women in leotards!

So when introducing relaxation as a necessary part of managing anger there is a need to be creative, to 'sell its benefits', even re-label it! It may help to consider the costs or effects of being tense and aroused in contrast to the benefits of being calm.

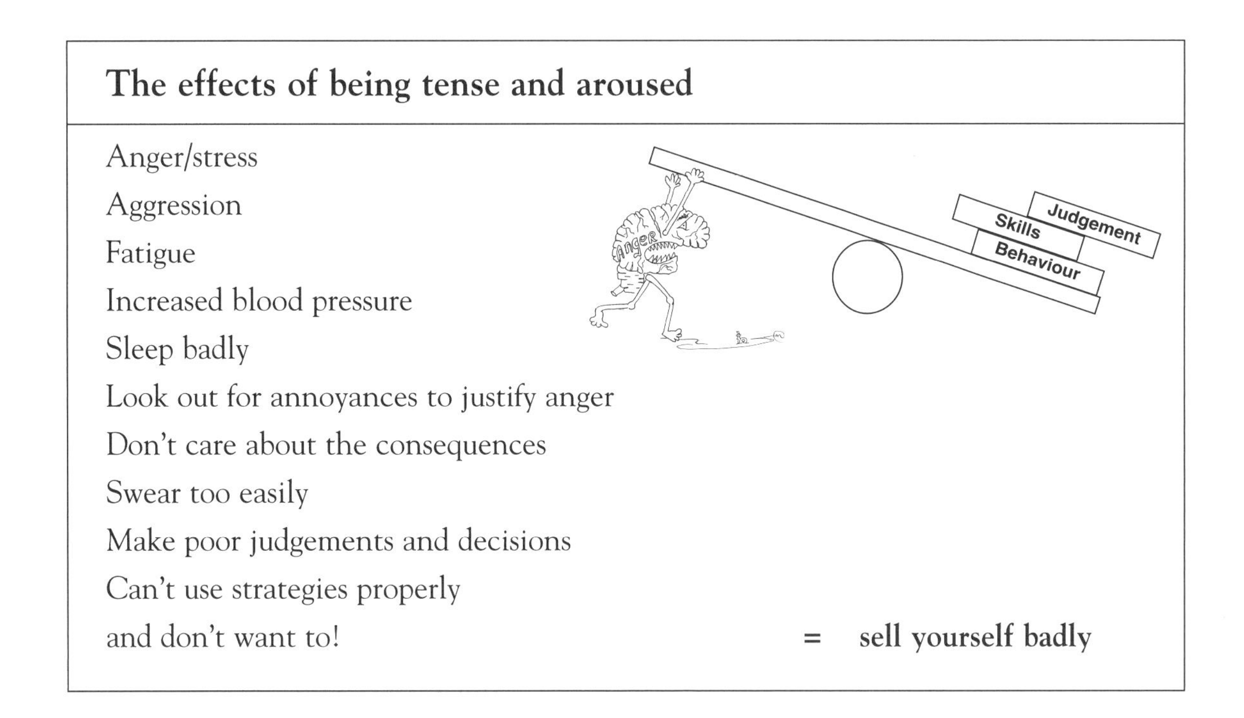

The effects of being tense and aroused

Anger/stress
Aggression
Fatigue
Increased blood pressure
Sleep badly
Look out for annoyances to justify anger
Don't care about the consequences
Swear too easily
Make poor judgements and decisions
Can't use strategies properly
and don't want to! = **sell yourself badly**

There are a variety of relaxation methods, all of which have their own theoretical backgrounds and have had a great deal written about them, including a thorough review by Payne (2000). When therapists teach relaxation techniques it is often their personal choice and experience that dictate which methods they use with clients. Nevertheless, ideally the therapist will be familiar with, and able to offer, alternative methods if a client has difficulty with the particular technique being used.

All methods of relaxation aim to reduce physiological arousal within the body. As this arousal is governed by the autonomic nervous system it is worth reminding ourselves of its role. The action of the *autonomic nervous system* is involuntary and designed to enable us to survive. It has two branches:

The sympathetic nervous system:
which prepares the internal organs for emergencies by producing changes known as the 'fight-flight' response. So when a person is, or perceives themselves to be, under threat, this system increases the activity of the heart and sends blood away from the internal organs to the voluntary muscles so that they are ready for action.

The parasympathetic nervous system:
which restores the body to a resting state in the absence of challenge, anger, fear or excitement. We know that slowed breathing is also associated with parasympathetic activity, so by making efforts to slow down the breathing rate it may be possible to counteract the effects of the sympathetic nervous system and arrest the symptoms of arousal. The relaxation response (Benson 1985) is an example of this. Hence the breath out is an important part of slowing down the symptoms of arousal, and many breathing techniques include a longer breath out than in, e.g. *breathe in for the count of* 4, *and out for the count of* 6. OTSAR is based on this theoretical concept and therefore always begins with a BREATHE OUT (see next page).

OTSAR or ON THE SPOT AROUSAL REDUCTION

O n

T he

S pot

A rousal

R eduction

WHAT IS OTSAR?

- It is a way of reducing levels of physiological arousal and body tension.
- It is a method that can be graded and therefore easily used anywhere, anytime.
- It has the potential to be customised to suit an individual's needs.

OTSAR COMBINES A NUMBER OF TECHNIQUES:

- breathing – this is a key point
- simple relaxation
- self-monitoring levels of arousal and measuring them by equating to a visual measure, e.g. the anger thermometer interrupting angry thoughts
- distraction techniques
- calming statements – what to do, feel or think
- imagery – some find this easier than verbal statements

Breathing

Start with breathing out – breathe away the anger! Often people are told to 'take a deep breath' but this is not helpful because:

1) This is associated with the 'fight-flight response' as in taking a deep breath before fighting or running because you are being chased!
2) A deep breath is not always a comfortable action to take at times of escalating anger when breathing is becoming increasingly shallow. To take in a deep breath at this point can give the feeling of bursting!

So BREATHE OUT first, before taking two complete deep breaths.

OTSAR IS INTRODUCED IN STEPS:

1. calming breaths
2. learning to self-monitor and differentiate between tense and relax
3. chair version – work progressively through the body
4. standing version
5. learning to turn it on/off anywhere, anytime!

OTSAR CAN HELP YOU TO

- Avoid getting really angry by short-circuiting anger arousal before it becomes too strong (because once we are 'up on the thermometer' it is really difficult to interrupt the escalation).
- Pay attention, listen and process information more effectively.
- Take a cool look at the situation, put it into context.
- Think clearly, decide what to do, ask for help if necessary.
- Use the anger productively to get something done, get confidence to use assertion.
- Perform better.
- Remember, the more angry you are the worse decisions you make!
- Build up a better track record.
- Feel calmer, and this helps your general health and stress levels.

WHEN TO USE IT

- When you feel the warning signs.
- When you know you are entering a situation that will probably annoy you
- Before being assertive.
- When the 'wind-up thoughts' begin to race.
- When you realise that your voice is getting louder or your gestures are getting bigger.
- Learn your triggers for anger and make them your triggers for OTSAR!

HOW TO LEARN OTSAR

- Step-by-step, starting with calming breaths. Please read on.

Step 1 of OTSAR – CALMING BREATHS

The first step of relaxation and arousal reduction is to become aware of the way we breathe, and to learn to look upon calming breaths as something that will help 'keep a lid on' the level of anger arousal.

Ideally these techniques should be learned whilst lying down, but if this is not popular, sit up straight in a chair. The therapist should first model how to take a deep breath properly, and then allow the individual to rehearse the technique.

Exercise

- Place one hand on your abdomen just above your waistline, and put the other on your chest.
- Breathe in your usual way and notice which hand rises when you take a breath in.
- Was it the one on your chest or on your abdomen? Most likely it was your chest and, if so, that means that you are breathing from your chest and using only the top space in your lungs (explain anatomy if appropriate). This happens more when you are angry or anxious and then it becomes more difficult to breathe properly.
- So the plan is to breathe so that the hand on your abdomen moves, and then we know you are filling the bottom part of your lungs, and breathing from your diaphragm.
- Take a long slow breath OUT and empty your lungs, then slowly breathe in and pull the air right down to the lower part of your lungs (your abdomen should rise, NOT your chest area), then as you continue to breathe in slowly bring the air up to your chest area. Hold for the count of 2 initially (later try for longer) then BLOW the air out through your mouth in one long slow breath.
- This may take time to practise.
- Later, the blowing out may be accompanied by a calming word, or a prompt from the coping card that is introduced in sessions 11/12.
- Once the technique of using the whole space in the lungs has been mastered, it can be used not only when the individual is lying down, but sitting, or standing. With practice, the technique can be carried out quite discreetly.

Step 2 of OTSAR – SELF-MONITOR/TENSE/RELAX

The second step means learning to self-monitor and differentiate between tense and relaxed muscles. It is important to appreciate what it feels like to be calm, because only then can a comparison be made. Clients often say *'Oh I'm OK I'm only 20% tense'*, but after relaxation they re-evaluate their rating and say *'Now I realise what it feels like to be calm, I think I must have been 50% tense'*.

This step can be achieved by following the principles of the well-known methods of relaxation that are listed below. It has not been possible to describe all of these and as explained earlier on page 21, many therapists are experienced in relaxation training and have determined which method is most suitable for their clients. However, if not, here is a list of recommended methods (all described by Payne 2000) that can allow the individual to learn the difference between being tense and relaxed.

Mitchell (1977)

Simple physiological relaxation – the procedure is to reposition joints and train the body to receive messages of comfort in a relaxed position.

Benson (1976)

The relaxation response based on meditative principles. It uses a simple repetitive mental device (word) to maintain attention.

Behavioural relaxation training (Schilling and Poppen 1983, Lindsay and Morrison 1996 or Poppen 1989)

Observable states of relaxation learned through observation and imitation.

Jacobson (1938)

Progressive relaxation which aims to recognise tension in the body and then to induce relaxation. However, this method can be very lengthy and a shorter version by Bernstein and Borkovec (1973) is described in Payne (2000).

TIP: Whichever method is used self-monitor before and after the relaxation. The key areas of the body to work on when angry are the:

- hands – no fists
- shoulders
- neck
- jaw.

REMEMBER: at the end of any relaxation or OTSAR allow time to come out of the relaxing state gently:

- Be aware of the sounds around you.
- Wiggle your fingers and toes.
- Open your eyes when you are ready.
- How do you feel? Where are you on the thermometer/scale?

Step 3 of OTSAR – SITTING VERSION

Use when angry or practise each day anyway.

- Find a chair and 'plonk yourself' down. Sit well back into the chair and rest your hands and arms on your thighs, or on the arms of the chair.
- Breathe OUT – blow away the anger (some people like to imagine blowing out a candle).
- Then breathe in through your nose, pushing out your tummy muscles and rib cage, breathe out through your mouth and relax; do this twice.
- Now take smaller breaths (or you will see stars) and concentrate on settling your body.
- Lift your heels and push your toes downwards, then rock back on your heels and lift your toes up, then repeat this once.
- Put both feet firmly on the ground so that they are well supported and then will not jiggle.
- Be aware of the chair under your legs and supporting your back.
- Arch your back, then push back into the chair, stop pushing and allow your bodyweight to sink into the chair.
- Stretch out your arms and spread your fingers apart. Now stop stretching and reposition your arms, then repeat.
- Push your shoulders down towards the floor, then stop pushing; if they jump back up towards your ears, then repeat this.
- Remember your breathing – in through your nose and out through your mouth.
- Allow your eyes to close gently and now let's settle your head.
- Allow it to roll very gently first to one side and then to the other.
- Now let your head find a comfy spot so that it can settle.
- Open your mouth slightly and wiggle your bottom jaw. Now stop, and close your lips but not your teeth. Swallow and allow your tongue to rest on the bottom of your mouth.
- Allow the lines and frowns to go from your face, to smooth away, up and over the top of your head.
- Remember your breathing – in through your nose and out through your mouth.
- Think of your calming statement, your prompt card or coping book. (Use this line only after session 11 when self-instruction is introduced.)

- Monitor your level of arousal – think of the thermometer.
- If you feel more calm and less angry and tense:

BE PLEASED WITH YOURSELF!
YOU KEPT A LID ON THINGS
WELL DONE!!

- Continue to breathe in peace and relaxation, and to breathe out the anger and tension.

TIP: It may help to include imagery of moving to a 'safe calming place' before starting

Step 4 of OTSAR – STANDING VERSION

Use when you start to feel the 'warning signs' of anger or tension. It is also a good idea to practise this daily whether you feel angry or not.

- Breathe out – blow away the anger.
- Breathe in through your nose and lift your shoulders up.
- Breathe out, push your shoulders down and stretch out your fingers.
- Breathe in through your nose.
- Breathe out and stop the stretching – allow your shoulders and arms to relax.
- Change your posture – break the tension lock – move your feet and stand tall, then stand still and relax.
- Remember the steady breathing – in through your nose and out through your mouth.
- Make sure your shoulders are down and that your arms are hanging loosely by your side.
- Open your mouth slightly and wiggle your bottom jaw. Now close your lips but not your teeth. Swallow and rest your tongue on the bottom of your mouth.
- Screw up your forehead, then relax – allow the lines to go from your face.
- Think of:
  - calming statement or scene
  - the gentle wind blowing in your hair
  - that scene of relaxation.
- Concentrate on something around you.
- Focus.
- Breathe regularly.
- Monitor your level of arousal – think of the anger thermometer.
- If you feel more calm, and less angry and tense:

BE PLEASED WITH YOURSELF!
WELL DONE!
YOU KEPT BELOW YOUR NE-NAR ZONE!

Step 5 of OTSAR – LEARNING TO TURN IT ON/OFF ANYWHERE, ANYTIME

The final stage of OTSAR is to apply the techniques 'on the spot' anywhere, anytime. It is a routine that can be used whenever there are warning signs of anger. It should include:

- breathing OUT
- addressing body tension in key areas – hands/fists, shoulders, neck, jaw.
- thought stopping and/or distraction
- calming statements and/or visualisation.

With practice this quick technique becomes a shortened and unobtrusive relaxation response. At a psychological level it is pairing specific thoughts with inducing a state of reducing physiological arousal. So in time and with practice the verbalising of relaxation self-statements should evoke the response.

CUSTOMISING OTSAR

The scripts for step 3, 4 and 5 can be customised for clients' individual needs and personal taste. Some clients prefer a recording of the spoken script which they can then use in their own time. This encourages the pairing of increasing arousal and the use of OTSAR. Discuss with the client whose voice they feel they will respond to. If they are able to read the script out themselves this may evoke less resentment than if they hear someone else prompting them; this is then a form of self-instruction.

Note: keep a master copy of the tape – it could get lost!

An example of a customised version of step 3

This individual had worked through the course and was able to use imagery and self-statements. He also:

- wore glasses
- could not breathe through his nose
- had a 'special' picture of a safe calm place.

Script – use when angry, but also practise each day.

- Find a chair and 'plonk yourself' down. Sit well back into the chair and rest your arms on your thighs, or on the arms of the chair.
- Take off your glasses and put them in a safe place.
- Breathe out – blow away the anger – think of your coping card and picture.
- Breathe in and out through your mouth, do this twice.
- Now take smaller breaths (or you will see stars) and concentrate on settling your body.
- Put both feet firmly on the ground so that they are well supported.
- Be aware of the chair under your legs and supporting your back.
- Allow yourself to sink into the chair.
- Breathe in, then as you breathe out push your shoulders down towards the floor.
- Breathe in and stop pushing; if your shoulders jump back up towards your ears then repeat this.
- Concentrate on the picture on your card, scan the outline of shapes.
- Allow your eyes to close, and now let's settle your head.
- Allow it to roll very gently first to one side and then to the other.
- Now let your head find a comfy spot so that it can settle.
- Remember your breathing – in and out through your mouth.
  Open your mouth slightly and wiggle your bottom jaw. Swallow and rest your tongue on the bottom of your mouth. Now close your lips but not your teeth.
- Screw up your eyes and nose, then stop and allow them to relax.
- Allow the lines and frowns to go from your face, to smooth away and drain away your tension.
- Remember your breathing – in and out through your mouth.
- Think of your calming statements on your prompt card.
- Monitor your level of arousal – think of the thermometer.
- If you feel more calm and less angry and tense:

BE PLEASED WITH YOURSELF!
WELL DONE!
THAT'S YOU TAKING CONTROL!
KEEP THE LID ON YOUR KETTLE!

- So breathe in peace and relaxation.
- Breathe out the anger and tension.
- You can hear sounds around you, but that's OK – they are not talking to you – you don't have to answer – just concentrate on cooling down, coming down the scale.
- Eyes are gently closed.
- Now think again about what made you angry.
- Are you sure you got the facts right? – listened properly?
- Was it worth getting angry? Maybe not…?
- But if it is something you have to sort out and talk about, you will do it better if you are calm.
- So breathe in and out through your mouth.
- Remember, you can only do your best!

At the end of OTSAR

- Be aware of the sounds around you.
- Wiggle your fingers and toes.
- Open your eyes when you are ready.
- How do you feel? Where are you on the thermometer/scale?

An example of a customised version of step 4

Cathy had a history of erratic verbal outbursts and impulsive behaviours. During treatment we had discovered that often her physiological arousal was initially accompanied by anxious and angry thoughts. She responded well to a system that interrupted and questioned her racing negative thoughts. Cathy did not always monitor her escalating arousal but gave her carers licence to gently prompt her to self-monitor by saying –

'Cathy what's your mercury level?'

Script – try and use this when you start to feel the warning signs of anger or stress. It is also a good idea to practise it daily whether you feel stressed or not.

Cathy you are getting near your Ne-Nar zone, so –

- STOP

- Breathe OUT – think of your thermometer
- Breathe in through your nose and bring your shoulders up
- Breathe out and push your shoulders down and stretch out your fingers
- Breathe in through your nose
- Breathe out and STOP stretching – allow your shoulders and arms to relax
- Now move gently and have a little stretch – then STOP, relax, and think of your thermometer (bet your mercury level has stopped going up!)
- Wiggle your bottom jaw and swallow
- Relax your face and breathe out slowly
- Remember you deserve to keep calm, then you are better at solving any problems you have

Once Cathy was familiar with this routine we designed a small coping card that she agreed to carry and use. This prompted her to question her racing thoughts.

So what is this about? – look at your card

Side 1

Is it a problem to solve

No → *Turn over*

Yes
↓

- Plan for it
- Do you need to get help?
- Talk it through
- Use the PSR

Side 2

- Are you stressed about something you can't fix?
- Or is it worth getting angry over?
- Maybe not ....?
- Use your OTSAR
- Get your head on something else

↓

If I feel more calm and less stressed, be pleased ....

It's a good feeling to be calm!

An example of a customised version of step 5

Dave had very high standards for both himself and others. We discovered that his NATS (negative automatic thoughts) were very inflaming and that he often experienced anger and a strong sense of injustice.

We wrote and taped Dave's voice to use as self-instruction.

- I'm getting wound up!
  Help I've got NATS! – Oooh, chuck them in the bin!

- Breathe out, then take a deep breath in.

- As you breathe out, push your shoulders down and stretch your fingers.
  Now relax and breathe in the calm.
  Breathe away the frustration – Remember blaming is inflaming!

- So I'm going to get calm then I can think clearly.
  If I need to be assertive I'll do a better job when I'm calm.

- It's a good feeling to be calm, WELL DONE!

Some do's and don'ts of relaxation and breathing techniques

Do:

- Remember relaxation is a skill that we have to learn (just like riding a bike!).
- Remember our bodies will not 'just relax' because we tell them to, just as our body does not 'get warm' on demand.
- Practise regularly.
- Find a quiet room with a bed, or a comfortable chair with a headrest.
- Later, try different positions, lying, sitting or standing.
- Undo any tight clothing such as a tie or belt, and remove spectacles.
- Use a personalized tape of the OTSAR script and music you like. Once you can manage the techniques you can use them anywhere; you do not have to have a darkened room or a mat. (The lack of these things has been given as a reason for not practising the techniques!)
- Allow time to 'come to' slowly in a quiet room, otherwise all the good work can be undone very quickly.
- Use OTSAR anytime, anywhere.
- Remember that gradually the relaxation response is triggered more speedily.

Don't:

- Practise full relaxation too soon after a meal; leave it for about an hour between eating and relaxing.
- A heavy smoker may have reduced elasticity of the lungs and therefore not be able to breathe deeply without coughing. Ask for medical advice if concerned.
- Try not to sleep when you are learning the techniques, you need to be awake to discriminate between tense and relaxed states.
- Sleeping does not prove that you are relaxed; we can all sleep when we are tense, hence those stiff necks in the morning!

The Anger Thermometer

The anger thermometer has proved to be useful when helping individuals to quantify their anger. It can be used both as a teaching aid and as a measurement tool for self-monitoring. Hence this follows the principles of cognitive behavioural work in a simplified form.

The wording used has evolved from user feedback. However, when individuals have their own set of labels that they prefer to use, they can design their own scale and therefore have a greater sense of ownership. Examples have been Stressometers, Arrrrrrrrrhometers, Stevometers, etc.; see examples on pages 182, 183.

The thermometer can be used in a variety of ways:

A large version on thick card, say 50 x 70cm, used:

- As a teaching aid. A session could be devoted to creating this scale which then belongs to the group (adolescents seem to like this).
- With colour added to the thermometer, i.e. red at the top (near boiling) and cool blue at the bottom; or red, amber and green to correspond with the traffic lights.

Small versions used as:

- A handout to increase awareness of anger arousal – useful to display as a prompt on the bedroom door or mobile phone, e.g. if you are above 30, don't dial!
- A self-monitoring sheet.
- A blank handout which can be customised to include the individual's own wording or pictures.
- As a picture in the individual's coping card/book.

ANGER THERMOMETER

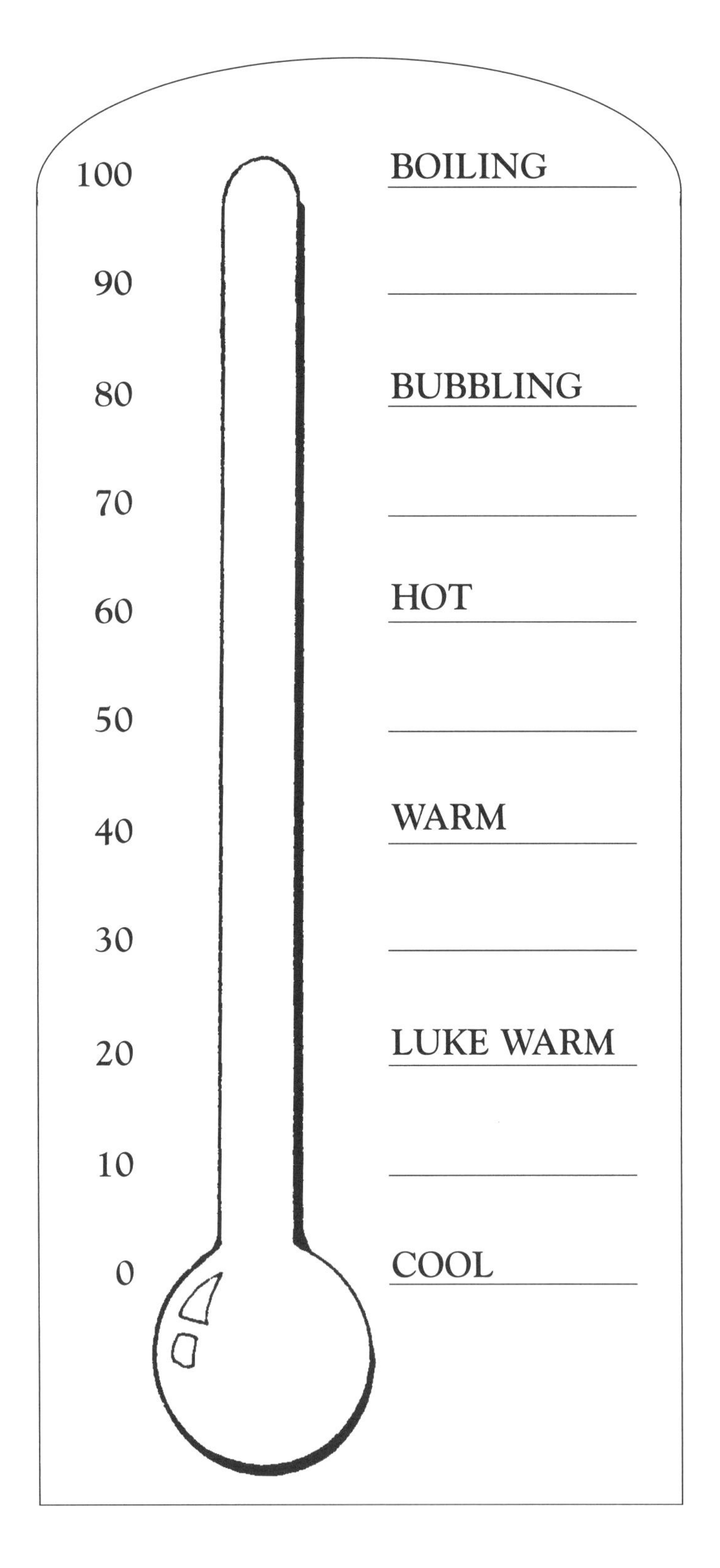

____________________THERMOMETER

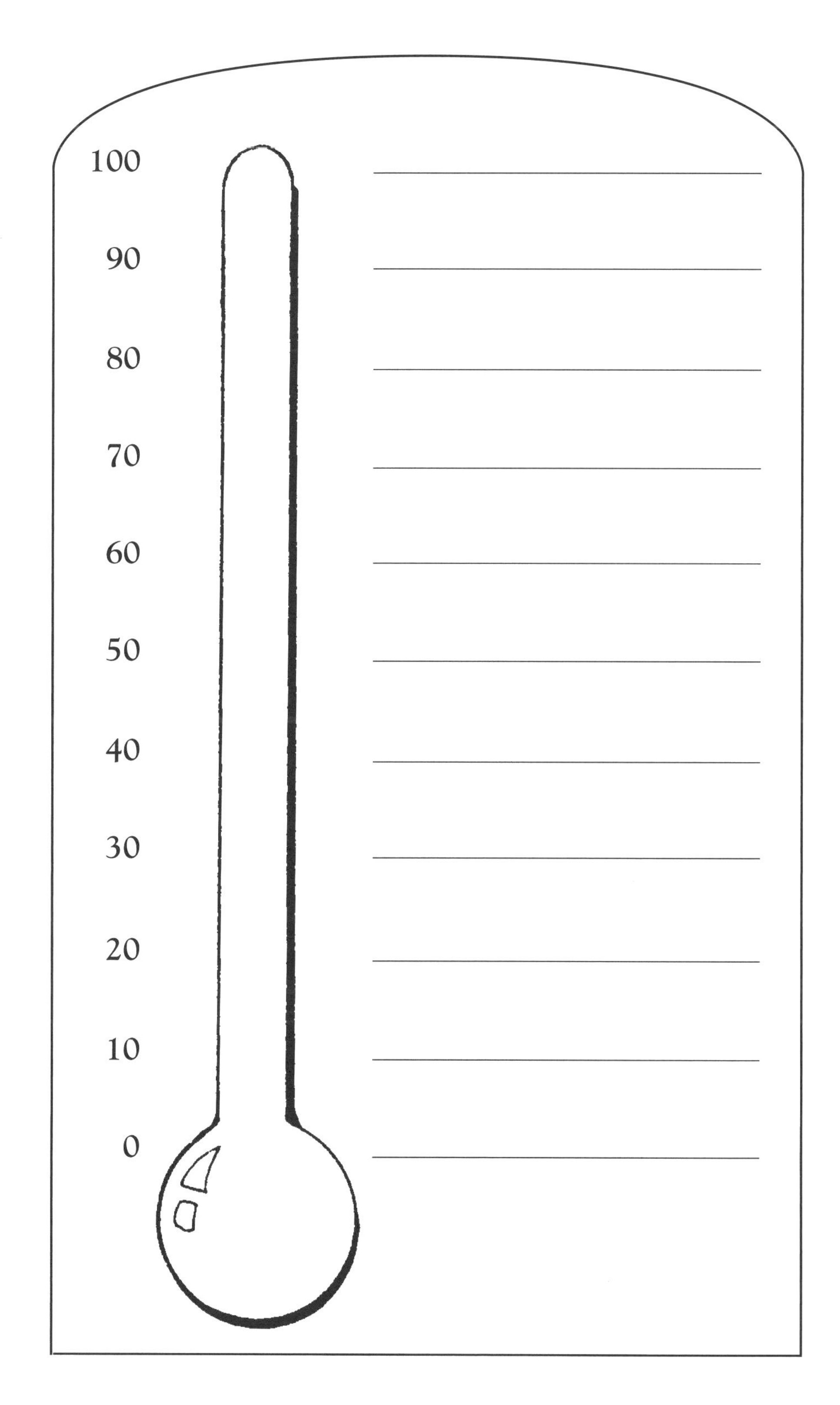

An example of an ARRRHOMETER

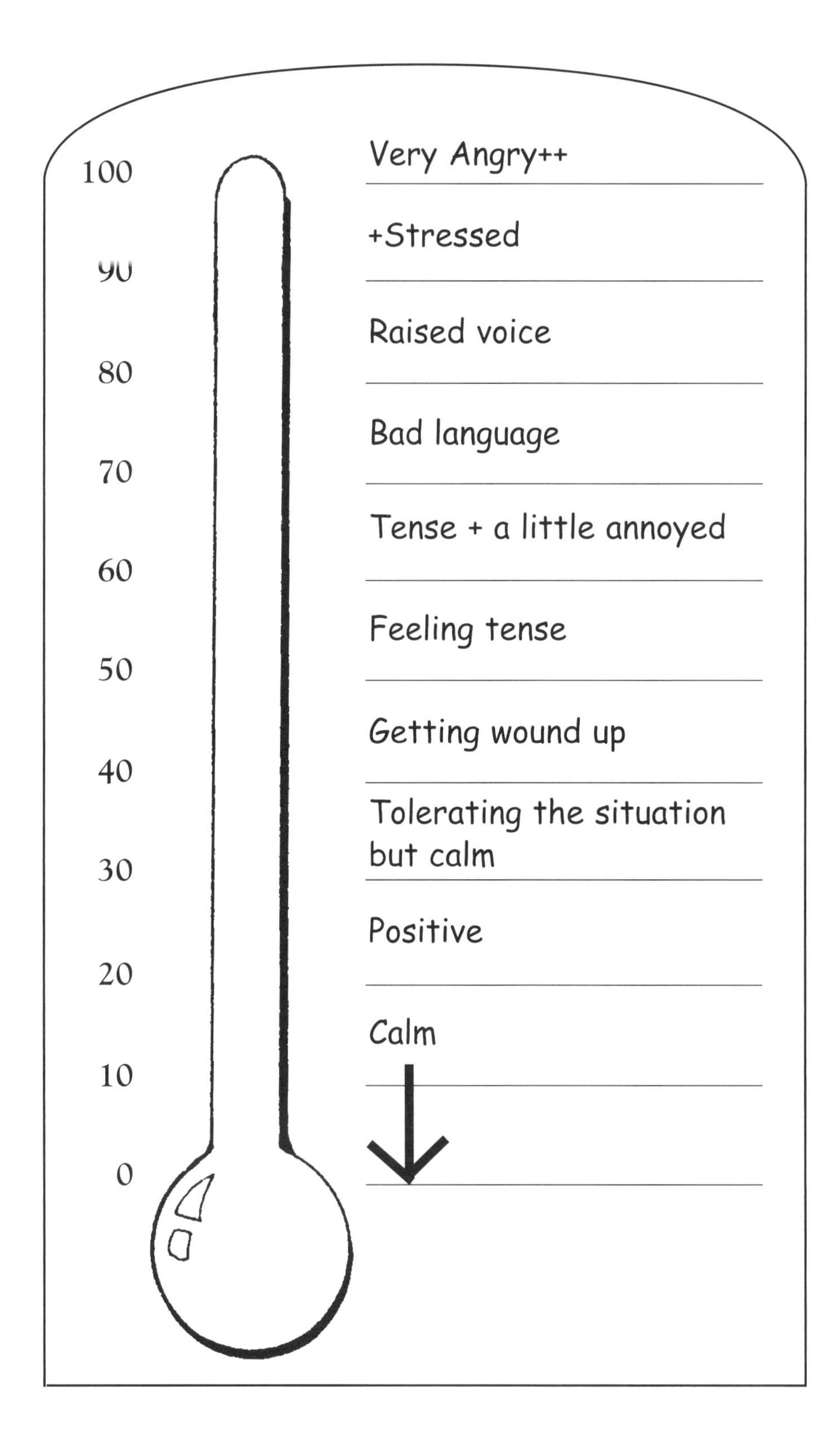

An example of a **STRESSOMETER**

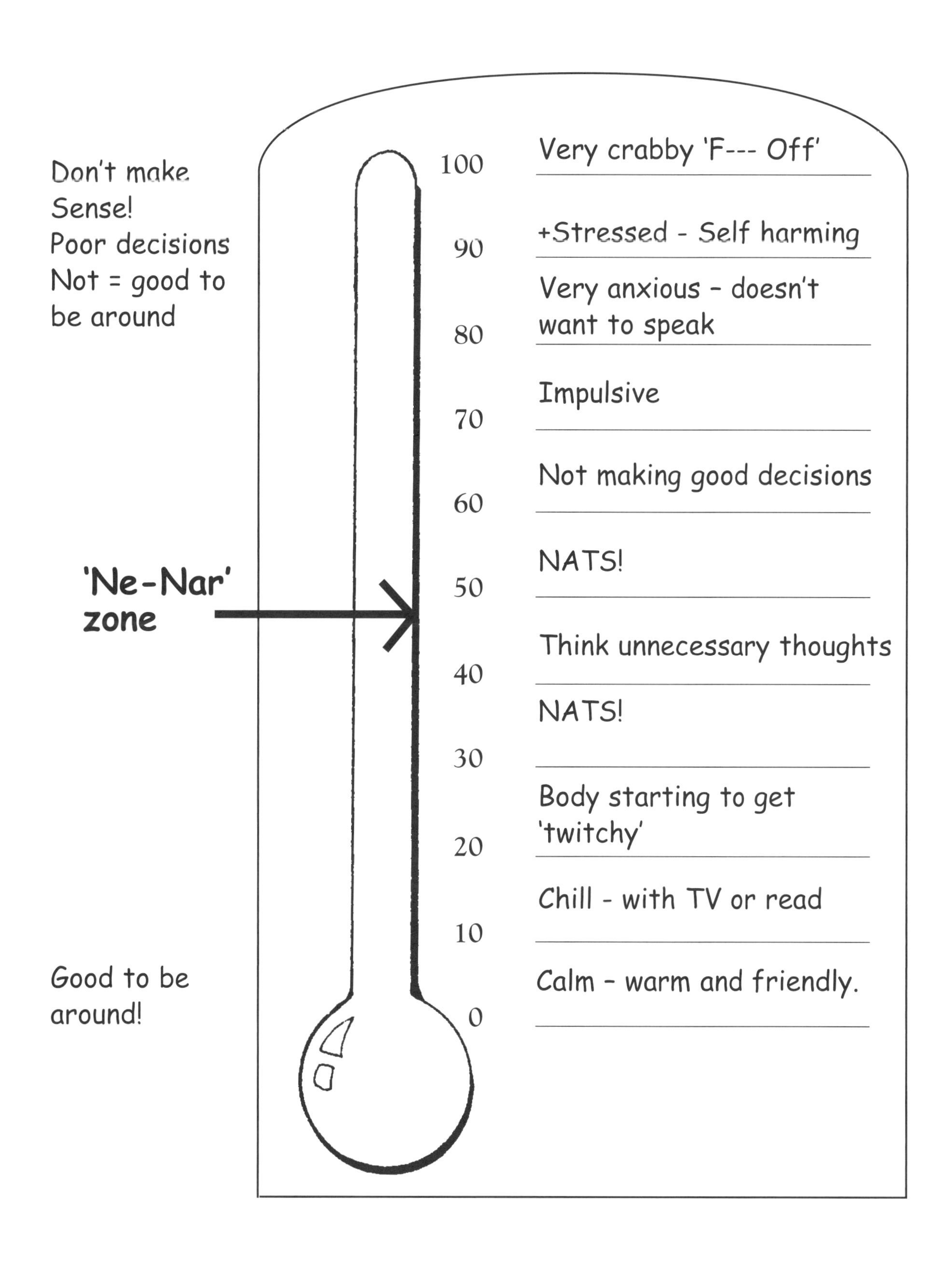

Re session 7 and after **Name** ______________________

Record of relaxation or OTSAR practice

Before you practise your relaxation or OTSAR:

1) STOP and think *where am I on my thermometer?*
2) Measure and make a note of the number.

Week beginning	Thermometer rating before practice	Thermometer rating after practice	Did you use any music?	Comments?
Day 1				
Day 2				
Day 3				
Day 4				
Day 5				
Day 6				
Day 7				

Please bring this sheet with you to the next session

OUTLINE OF A PERSON

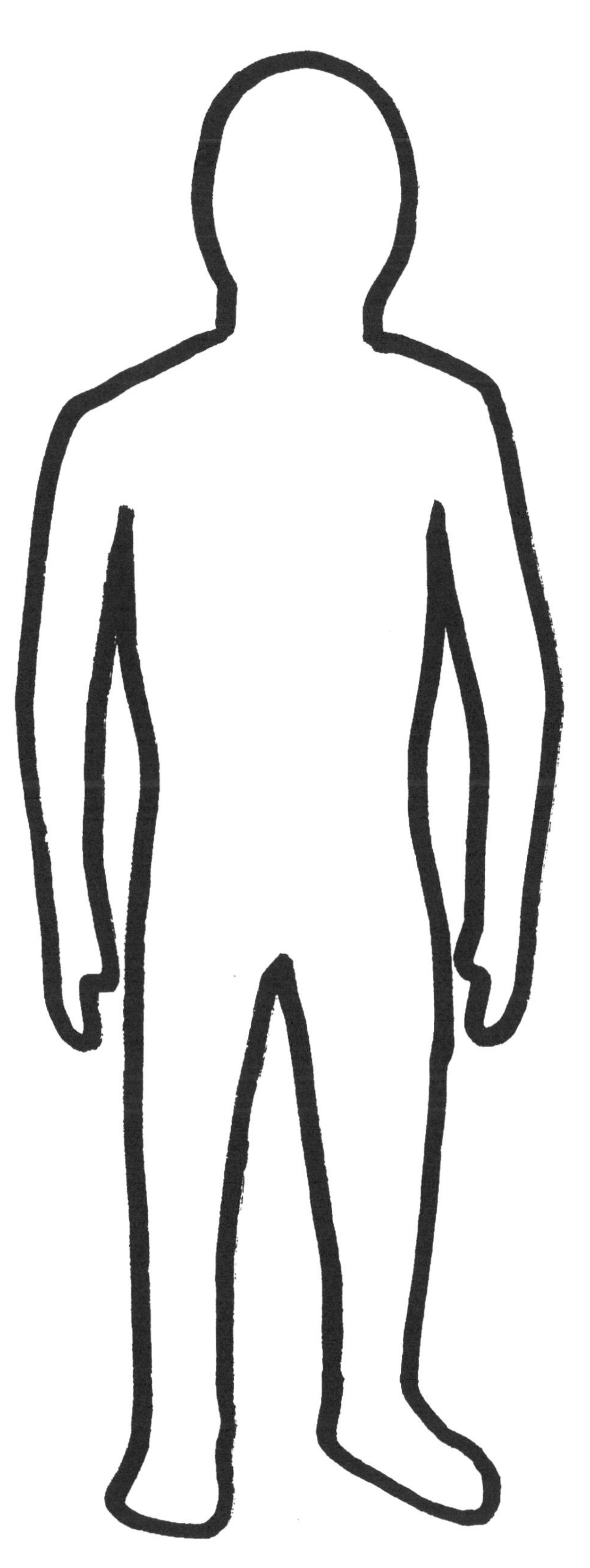

APPENDIX 2

THE COGNITIVE COMPONENT

GENERAL COPING SELF-STATEMENTS

These are examples of coping or positive self-statements. However, they are not just the opposite of negative statements, but are a self-instruction to either take an action or view a situation differently. They can be used in Session 9 to contrast the 'wind-up' thoughts, and for self-instruction. This is a general list and is offered for those individuals whose discriminatory powers or memory do not allow them to use the four stages of S.I.T. and for whom it is advisable to stick to a general statement that can be used at any time.

These self-statements should not be presented to the client for them just to pick one. It is ideal if they can produce their own meaningful statements, perhaps a helpful statement that others have said to them. So ask what a trusted elder or friend would say: *You say your Gran always helped calm you down, what would she have said to you?*

Here are some examples that others have found useful:

- It's challenge time – relax.
- Don't let it get to you.
- My muscles are getting tight, time to relax and slow things down.
- Relax I can solve this, but think before I do or say anything.
- Don't take it personally.
- Breathe away the anger.
- Breathe deeply and slowly.
- It's time to breathe out and stretch your jaw.
- My anger is a sign that I need to use my card.
- Just listen to yourself! You are taking yourself up the wall – chill.

- Speak slowly and quietly, don't yell.
- Listen to what they have to say, give them a chance!
- Don't give them the satisfaction of seeing you angry.
- Don't get carried away.
- It won't kill me to do it.
- Ignore them, don't get involved, it's not worth it.
- Control and focus!
- Think of my goals.
- Did I listen properly and get the whole story?
- It's not worth a fight, I can't always win.
- Some things even I can't solve.
- Who says we have to agree?
- It's not fair, but losing my temper will just make things worse.
- Can't win 'em all!

Beware – strategies and statements need to reflect individuality

People are sometimes advised to use counting as a distraction, or to pace their breathing and this can be helpful. However:

- ensure that the client can count fluently or this will be provocative to them
- a suggestion to count backwards from 10–0 whilst imagining the mercury level dropping on the thermometer, has been helpful for many; but one lady said it reminded her of countdown before 'Blast-off'.

COPING OR POSITIVE SELF-STATEMENTS (FOUR STAGES)

Examples of self-statements are given for each of the four stages in the sequence of anger arousal. A general list has also been given for those individuals whose discriminatory powers do not allow them to select which statement to use at which time.

STAGE 1: PREPARING FOR PROVOCATION

- Breathe out and relax, you'll think more clearly.
  STOP, Think, Plan

- I'll be prepared. If I start to lose it I'll check myself, I've got my routine.
- Remember what you are trying to sort out, stick to that.
- If I explain quietly they may listen.
- There won't be any need for an argument.
- This is going to upset me, but I can deal with it.
- Easy does it, try not to take it too seriously.
- Stop worrying. Worrying won't help anything.
- This is a challenge – relax!

STAGE 2: DURING THE EVENT

- OK Ne-Nar, it's starting, but I'm ready for it.
- As long as I am cool I am in control.
- I don't have to prove myself.
- There's no point in getting cross/angry.
- It's a shame that he/she has to act like this; they must be very unhappy.
- I'm not going to let him/her get to me!
- Big slow breaths, stay focused, it will pass.

STAGE 3: COPING WITH AROUSAL

- Time to take a big breath out.
- My anger is a warning sign, I need to move away and relax.
- This is a warning sign, I need to use my coping statements/card/etc.
- Shoulders down, and stretch out your fingers.
- Take it easy, don't get pushy.
- Hey let it drop, think of tomorrow or your calming scene.

STAGE 4 : LEAVING THE ANGER AND LOOKING BACK

- I did my best and handled it OK.
- It wasn't as bad as I had thought.
- It's not fair, but losing my temper just makes things worse.
- I didn't win but I tried.
- That was a challenge, now relax!
- Good, I did it! Next time I'll do even better!
- I didn't get angry!

ADDITIONAL EXERCISES FOR COGNITIVE WORK

USE OF RECORDED TV SOAPS OR DRAMAS

- Record a TV programme that involves interpersonal situations leading to disagreement.
- Allow the group to watch the recording. Then ask them to go to different areas of the room and write down, or orally report to a scribe, their understanding of the situation that they saw.
- This provides some understanding of how the individuals have observed and interpreted the behaviour of others, and then appraised the situation. Discuss how easy it is to misunderstand situations. Refer to the styles of thinking on page 114, then notice how some people:

  – are always 'getting the wrong end of the stick'
  – are on the look-out for annoyances (expecting trouble)
  – focus on what might be wrong about a situation – rather than what was OK (mental filter)
  – overgeneralise – if one thing goes wrong it seems to them that everything always goes wrong. Is there any evidence?
  – jump to conclusions before they know the facts (mind reading)
  – are quick to label others or themselves – *he's a ...... fool, I'm a loser* instead of *I made a mess of it today*. These character labels are 'wind-up' statements and do not encourage logical discussion
  – blame others for their behaviour – this is a misattribution
  – use a lot of 'should' statements – this sets them up for anger and frustration.
    If they are aimed at themselves it can lead to resentment or even guilt (dictatorial thinking).

Should, ought and must are said to be illogical rules! In cognitive therapy they are thought of as one of the cognitive biases or Musterbations (Ellis, in Ellis and Tafrate 1997).

- All of these points can be used to provide a role-play of alternative endings to scenarios.

IT'S EASY TO LET YOUR THOUGHTS 'WIND YOU UP'

- At times we all get rapid thoughts rolling over in our heads.
- It is definitely worth being aware of this because it can lead us to draw the wrong conclusion and then get angry or worried unnecessarily.
- Wind-up thoughts seem to make so much sense at the time!
- As thoughts race, body arousal increases, and visa versa.
- Rolling thoughts can be interrupted, stopped and challenged.

An example of the problems of the rolling thoughts!

A client had lots of questions about his future community placement and benefits. He made frequent phone calls to his social worker and to his key worker. He was given answers to some of his questions but others were not readily available. On a bad day, when the client had spent a long time worrying about his unknown future, his thoughts became progressively more and more distorted, his arousal level increased as did his sense of injustice. He was going to find out what was going on! He phoned his social worker only to be told she was out (she had popped out of the office to buy a sandwich for lunch). The client's rolling thoughts were as follows:

She's not in again! she's never in when I want her, she doesn't care about me! might as well not have a social worker, I'll never get my future sorted out! nothing ever works out for me there's no point in staying on here, I'm going to discharge myself, I'm going to leave!

When looking at the straight facts of the scenario it seems that the client was going to discharge himself, all because his social worker has gone out to buy a sandwich! Does that make sense? **Discuss.**

TRYING TO SEE IT FROM THE OTHER PERSON'S POINT OF VIEW

Trying to see the situation from the other person's point of view, or role-taking, can be a useful exercise. As an angry incident has been reported in a session: Try to get an accurate picture of the scenario.

- Set up a role-play to re-enact the scenario. Ask the angered person to take the part of him/herself, and reliable others to take other roles.
- After the role-play try to identify what the angry person was thinking as

they were angry. These thoughts may be unrealistic or illogical but they were real at the time, so don't dismiss them; empathise instead.

- Now swap roles and repeat the role-play, with the angered person now playing the provocative one.
- Any feedback from the participants? Did the angered person gain any new understanding of the situation? Was there an alternative explanation for the person's behaviour? Discuss how things are not always what they first seem!
- If any labelling took place – *he's a failure*! Look more carefully at the scenario and allow the client to explore whether they were basing that label on one mistake rather than a general comment. If so, a helpful reappraisal would be – *he got it wrong this time but he's not a failure as a person.*
- Try to challenge the individual's appraisal of the situation, if necessary.
- Use the opportunity to teach additional assertion and problem-solving skills.

What are your Rules for Life, and do they work?

We all have a set of rules for life. We adopt them as we are growing up and often they are very helpful, keep us out of trouble, and give us standards to live up to. However, some of these rules are so rigid they set us up to fail or get annoyed very easily, for example:

- I must always get things right.
- People who ask for help are wimps!

If someone follows these rules, or holds these assumptions, there is a danger that they would struggle to cope if they did need help. They would find it hard to ask for help and, if they did, they might be unforgiving and angry with themselves! These assumptions can be absolute and unconditional, e.g.:

- People should never be late!

Or conditional, e.g.:

- Unless I'm on my guard all the time people will take advantage of me.

Examples of other rules commonly held:

- If I apologise people will think I am backing down.
- People must do what they say they will do.

Can you think of any more?

Now take one such rule and try to work out the advantages and disadvantages of following it.

Example

People shouldn't be lazy!

Advantages	**Disadvantages**
Gets lots done	Don't relax
Maintains a high standard	Can get very tired
I feel good with myself	Might get crabby
It stretches me	When I say it to others they think I'm very bossy and a swot
I like to be busy	I expect everyone else to be busy and so I try to impose it on others
	Makes me unpopular if I do

- Discuss if it actually works.
- Is it worth following, or is it a hindrance rather than a help?
- Is the rule realistic? – would other people try to follow it? – ask them.
- Can you think of a replacement rule that might be less rigid and therefore kinder to you because it will not set you up for blaming others or yourself?

  e.g.: It's good to work hard, but it's okay to take a break.

- Now work through some of the other rules, or better still – think of your own. See the worksheet on page 240. If the client is able to rate how much they believe in that life rule, then ask them to do so before the advantage/disadvantage exercise above. After the exercise repeat the belief rating and compare to the original, it may have reduced slightly.

This is a way of shifting rigid rules or assumptions; but it is not a 'quick fix'. See examples of other modified rules below.

Original, Rigid, Prim and Proper Rules	**Advantages of this way of thinking**	**Disadvantages of this way of thinking**	**Modified Rules – more realistic helpful expectations**
People shouldn't interfere when I'm doing a job	They can't take over and leave me feeling inadequate	This sets me up for a lot of anger as sometimes I need help. I feel like crap for the rest of the day and my head is full of 'I can't do it'	I like it when people leave me alone to concentrate and get on. Sometimes I do need help so it's OK for people to offer help, I can always politely refuse
People shouldn't be rude!	Keeps standards of politeness An ideal to be aimed for	Get real! There ARE a lot of rude people around and I can't change that	I don't <u>like</u> it when people are rude and I can assert that if I choose to. I can make sure I'm not rude, but I can't insist that others follow my standards
I need to blow to get my point across	Dad used to do it, and it makes my daughter listen to me	People are scared of me and I don't want that – it's not the kind of attention I want	People are more likely to take notice and respect me if I plan, and then assert myself

Identifying a more reasonable and modified rule is only step one. Given that the person will have held the belief for a long time it will take time and work by the person themselves, and perhaps support and reminders, to change it.

BUBBLE PICTURE

BUBBLE PICTURE

HELPFUL CALMING THOUGHTS

HELPFUL CALMING THOUGHTS

'WIND UP' THOUGHTS

'WIND UP' THOUGHTS

THE THINK → FEEL → DO SEQUENCE

THE THINK → FEEL → DO SEQUENCE

THE THINK → FEEL → DO SEQUENCE

THE THINK → FEEL → DO SEQUENCE

THE THINK → FEEL → DO SEQUENCE

ANSWERING YOUR ANGRY THOUGHTS

ANSWERING YOUR ANGRY THOUGHTS

TAKE ANOTHER LOOK AT THE SITUATION THAT MADE YOU ANGRY

QUESTIONS TO ASK – if looking back at your diary or – rethinking the situation

1. Was the initial reason for the anger justified?

   - If so, think about this.
   - Was there some other possible reason for the situation?
   - Was there a misunderstanding?
   - Did you pick up the wrong signs?
   - Did you listen properly?
   - Did you 'get the wrong end of the stick'?

2. What were the unhelpful 'wind-up' thoughts?

3. Did they fuel the anger?

Try to think of more constructive useful thoughts to use another time. Write some down on the blank column on your diary, e.g.:

Instead of: *Why is she doing this to wind me up, it's always the same!*

Try: *Hey, I have a choice; I'm not going to let her get to me! This is a hassle-free zone!*

STARTING TO FEEL ANGRY?

QUESTIONS TO ASK YOURSELF

- Have I listened properly?
- Have I got the facts right?
- Have I got the whole story?
- Am I tired and irritable?
- Should I ask for more explanation?
- Is it worth getting angry over?
  Get calm.

CHALLENGING STATEMENTS AND QUESTIONS

- Maybe there's been a mistake.
- Have I checked there is no other reason for this situation?
- Have I explained myself clearly?
- I jumped in very quickly.
- Will this seem as important in a week's time? – or even an hour?
- If I do need to deal with it, I'll do it when I'm calm.

  Get calm – remind yourself of your goals.

Therapist's notes

Tiredness and fatigue can lead to irritability and anger. Many mental health clients describe such experiences which can be problematic and feed crabbiness. However, fatigue and loss of stamina are particularly limiting, and have to be respected by those who have suffered a brain injury (Powell 2004). Learning to anticipate and manage fatigue is a necessary part of emotional and behavioural management.

Introduce the P words! – then you won't need to use the F words!!

See handout on next page.

The secret is with the P words!
– then you won't need to use the F words!!

- **Plan**
- **Pace**
- **Prioritise**
- **Prepare**
- **Practice**
- **Purrrrrrrrrrrrrfect**

Plan what you are going to do and put it in the diary or on the calendar

Pace yourself – have regular breaks. Make sure you have some peaceful times. Respectfully assert your needs for space or a rest

Prepare as much as you can for things beforehand so that there is not a stressy last-minute rush – e.g. pack your bag in the evening ready for when you go out the next day

Practise any new skills or jobs, and be more confident

- Then you are more likely to be **Purrrrrrrrrrrrrfect!** Well almost!
- Remember realistic expectations are best
- Avoid the F words – Forget, Flustered, Fatigue or swearing!
- Be pleased with yourself = achieve and self-congratulate

GETTING TO KNOW YOUR ANGRY THOUGHTS

FACTS:

1) Often they are automatic and just fly into our heads. We do not have to look for them, they just come!

2) These **N**egative **A**utomatic **T**houghts are also called **NATS**; Help – I've got NATS!!

3) Tick which of these statements are about your angry thoughts

- They wind me up!
- They tend to lead to other similar thoughts – then I'm on a roller!
- They are personal to me
- They give me a strong message
- I really believe them!
  They make me rehearse my anger!
- It is worth learning to spot them then I can try and arrest them
- But they **are** hard to stop!

4) So we all get NATS at times, don't feel too bad about having them

Write down examples of your angry thoughts in the space below:

5) The trick is to learn to spot them, and then keep them 'in check' or challenge them
6) Because they **do** affect our mood and behaviour

DECIDE TO CHANGE WHAT YOU THINK OR SAY TO YOURSELF

Learn to notice or spot those negative 'wind-up thoughts'

Write them down or tape them whilst you are feeling angry

Then STOP and THINK and ask yourself:

- What are these doing to me?
- Am I rehearsing my anger?
- Can anything actually change?
- What must I sound like?
- Will this seem as important in a week's time – or even an hour?
- These thoughts are taking me up the wall!

I'm going to take charge of them

Chuck them in the bin ....

- Then think about getting calm
- If there is a problem to sort out, I'll do it when I'm calm.

APPENDIX 3

THE BEHAVIOURAL COMPONENT

ASSERTION TRAINING

Learning to be assertive is an important part of anger management training. Like all of the other components, assertion training can be graded according to the individual's capability. Sessions 19–21 explain the meaning of the assertive way compared to that of being aggressive or passive, also see The Assertive Way handout on pages 218 and 219. Simple examples of the different behaviours may have to be given to help clarify the meanings of 'even more long words'!

For further reading on assertiveness see Holland and Ward (2001), Powell (1992, 2001).

Discuss the differing consequences of being assertive, aggressive or passive, for example:

- Often the passive person feels angry a lot of the time.
- The aggressive person may well lose friends.
- The assertive person feels pleased with themselves for trying.
- A poor self-esteem is associated with those who show either passive or aggressive behaviours.

So being assertive means saying clearly what you want, need and/or feel, whilst at the same time respecting the needs, wishes and feelings of others. It means putting your point and needs across to others:

- saying clearly what you want or need
- saying it in a way that means business
- being able to say NO if you want to
- saying what you want to say, and feeling better because you have 'said your piece', even if it doesn't change anything!
- having respect for others and yourself
- taking responsibility for your own actions and choices.

Examples of assertive statements

- *I feel annoyed because your loud music is bothering me. Please turn it down.*
- *No, I just do not lend money to other people.*
- *Could you please put the cigarette out, it bothers me.*
- *Please can we talk about this and sort it out.*
- *When you said that I felt criticized, did you mean it that way?*
- *I am sorry you are upset, can we make up?*
- *When you said that it hurt my feelings*
- *I know we have different views on this. I'll listen to your point, you listen to mine and then we can agree to disagree!*

Being assertive is useful in situations such as:

- saying no
- making requests
- giving criticism
- receiving criticism
- stating opinions
- explaining dissatisfaction
- leaving a situation when you want to – exit skills
- explaining that there has been a mistake
- dealing with 'wind-ups'
- defending yourself against criticism
- expressing your own particular needs, e.g. to move from a busy setting before conversation so as to allow information to be processed more effectively
- asking others to do their share
- refusing unwanted help

- refusing an unwanted invitation
- getting the wrong change
- explaining that your benefits are late
- apologising
- agreeing to disagree with others (e.g. over football teams)
- explaining you don't like the other person switching a video on when you are watching the TV
- your neighbour is playing very loud music!
- asking a favour
- when given an incorrect order in a restaurant or shop
- being short-changed
- explaining a mistake at work
- interrupting and joining in with the crowd.

OUR RIGHTS TO BE ASSERTIVE

We all have certain basic human rights. If we are assertive we learn to stand up for those rights but still respect the rights of others. We do not push our opinions on others, that would be aggressive behaviour.

The Rights Charter

I have the right to:

- be treated with respect as an equal human being
- express my opinions, thoughts and feelings
- say *yes* and *no* for myself
- make reasonable requests of others and respect their response
- express my needs such as *I didn't catch that, sorry could you say it again,* or *Please could we move to a quieter place to speak*
- make mistakes and feel comfortable about admitting them
- recognise, respect and manage my fatigue and/or pain
- recognise that I am not responsible for other people's behaviours
- have a range of feelings and emotions but to 'let go' of some of my grief from the past
- I have the right to have hope for the future!

THE ASSERTIVE WAY

THE ASSERTIVE WAY

WERE YOU ASSERTIVE THIS WEEK?

Date

Situation

What did you do or say?

What did the other person do or say?

How did the situation end up?

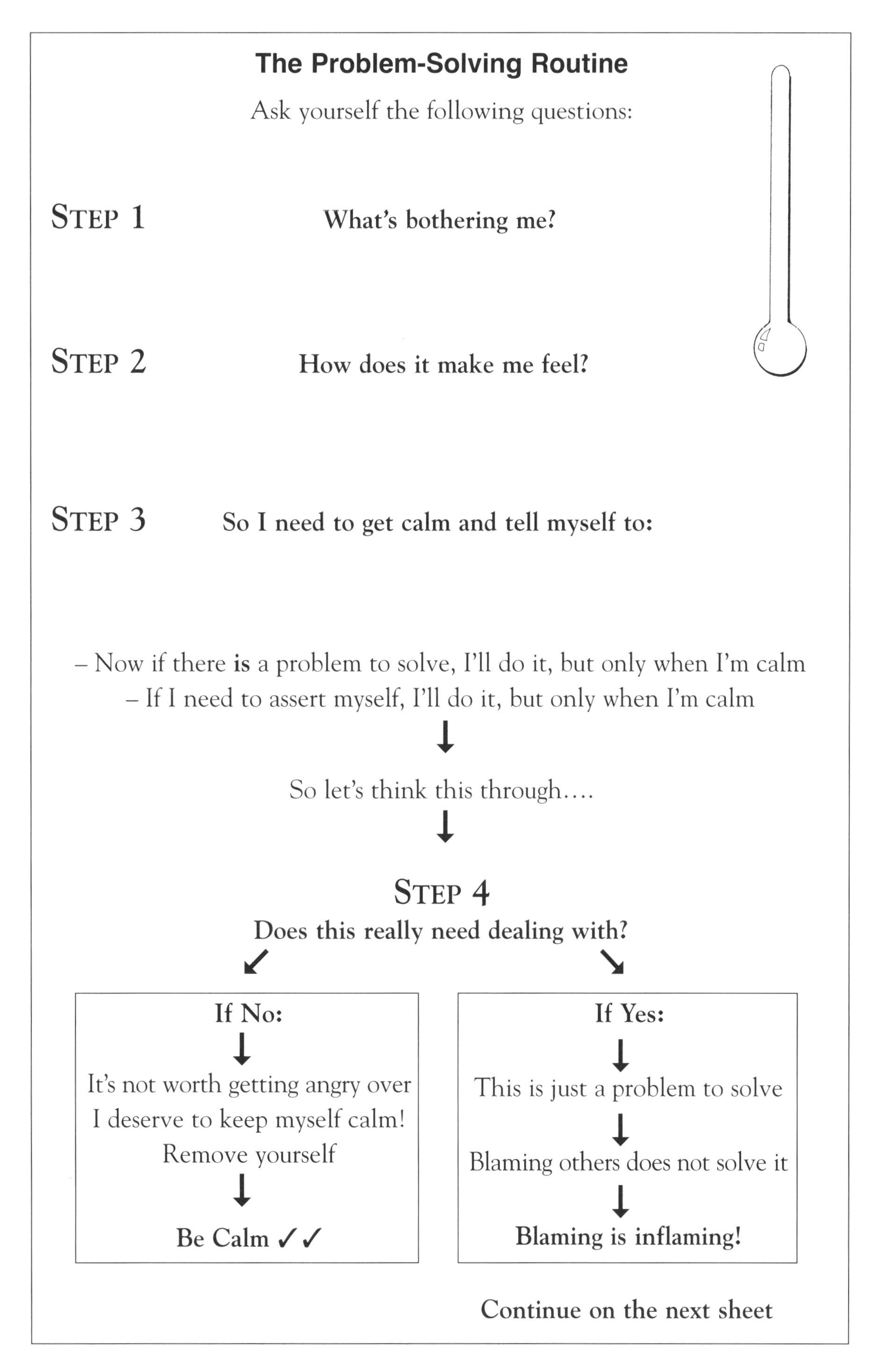

The Problem-Solving Routine

Ask yourself the following questions:

STEP 1 **What's bothering me?**

STEP 2 **How does it make me feel?**

STEP 3 **So I need to get calm and tell myself to:**

– Now if there **is** a problem to solve, I'll do it, but only when I'm calm
– If I need to assert myself, I'll do it, but only when I'm calm

↓

So let's think this through....

↓

STEP 4

Does this really need dealing with?

If No:	**If Yes:**
↓	↓
It's not worth getting angry over I deserve to keep myself calm! Remove yourself	This is just a problem to solve
↓	↓
	Blaming others does not solve it
	↓
Be Calm ✓✓	**Blaming is inflaming!**

Continue on the next sheet

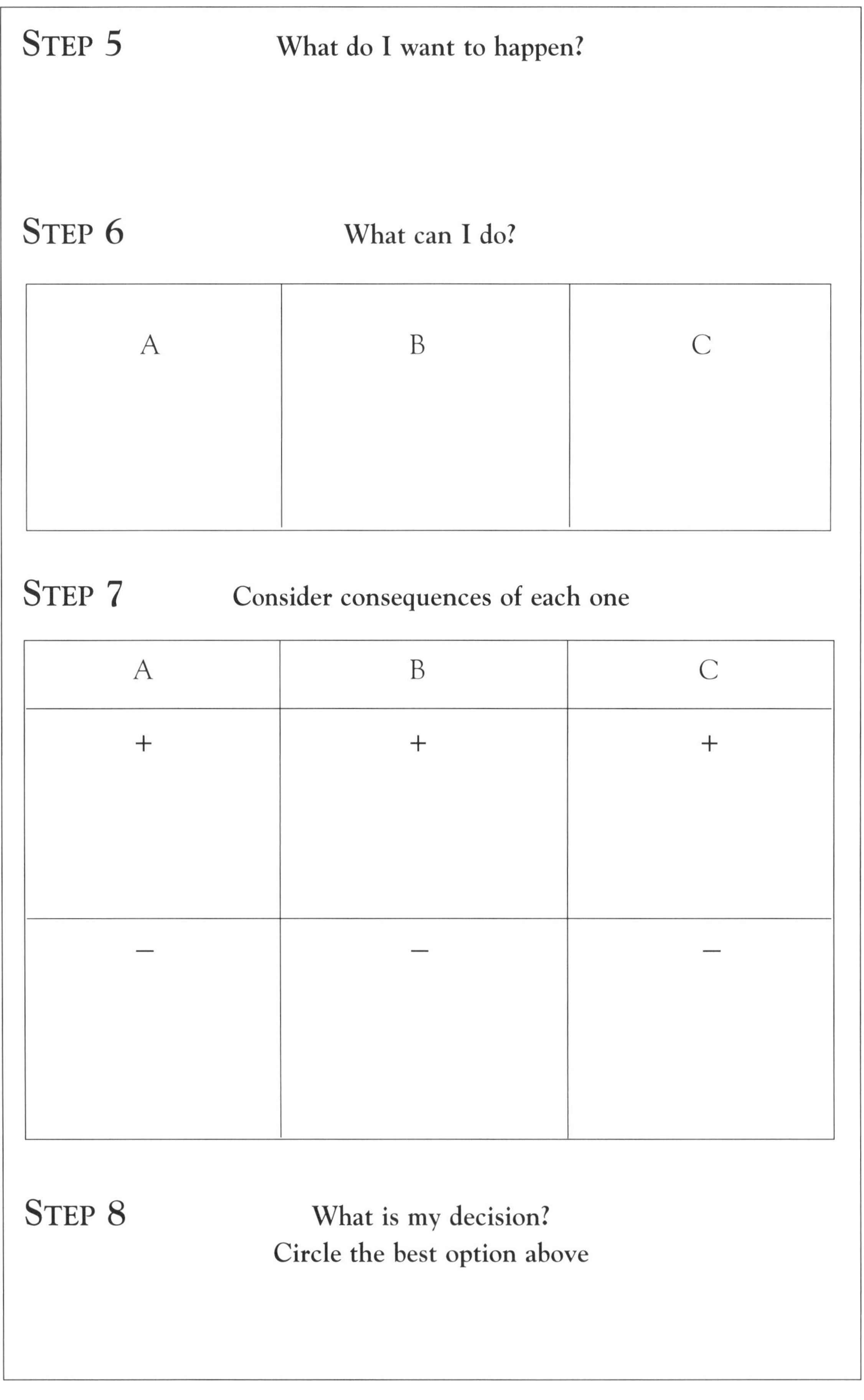

Step 5 What do I want to happen?

Step 6 What can I do?

A	B	C

Step 7 Consider consequences of each one

A	B	C
+	+	+
–	–	–

Step 8 What is my decision?
Circle the best option above

STEP 9 Plan how to carry this out

STEP 10 Now do it!

STEP 11 How did it work?

APPENDIX 4

DIARIES AND WORKSHEETS

There is unlimited scope for the design of diaries. A selection is provided in this appendix. They are listed in a progression, i.e. the early ones being more useful in the early part of the course.

The **WIND-UP SCALE** offers the opportunity to record a number (0–10, or 0–100) three times a day. This is so called for people who do not get angry but just get wound up! It needs to be accompanied by a measure, i.e. a personalized thermometer.

For some clients it is helpful to make recordings more frequently, say on an hourly basis. This can highlight any patterns of arousal or fatigue; or correlations with a particular time of day or activities on the timetable.

The **RECORD OF EMOTIONS** is used whilst learning to differentiate between emotions. Simple drawings, photographs, cut-out pictures or colours can be used as codes.

The **ANGER DIARIES** initially record information about 'the incident' and later involve information on arousal and the cognitive aspects. You will notice that the first version which records the three components of anger – Thinking, Feeling and Doing – does not follow the sequence. Instead it is printed in the order – Feeling, Thought and Behaviour. This is because recording one's thoughts is usually considered more difficult than recording bodily feelings. If the client cannot fill in the first column he/she may well 'file it in the bin', thus reducing the likelihood of compliance with diaries. The second version of the cognitive-behavioural diary does follow the correct sequence, and the third version has an additional column in which to challenge and re-appraise thoughts.

The sheet – Filling out an anger diary – asks questions that may prompt the client to reflect on the incident and state relevant details.

Decide with the client where to keep the used diaries and who will have access to them. Diaries will contain information about others which, if read out of context, could be misconstrued or cause offence. Contents of diaries are not necessarily facts, but they felt real to the client at the time of writing them! Therefore, if other staff are going to access the diaries do remind them not to react defensively if they find damning information about themselves. Any such defensive reaction will in turn inhibit the client's future recording. Having said this, there is always the client who uses the diary as a way to shock!

The **TRAFFIC LIGHT ROUTINE** can be a useful visual prompt. We are tuned to notice a red light and hence it may be a helpful way to gain the client's attention. This can be coupled with self-instructions. An example of a general script, a worksheet and an individualised script are included. Some clients chose to colour the traffic lights as well as their anger thermometer.

A variety of WORKSHEETS are included to offer choice and suitability for differing needs and appeal.

- **Ways to calm**
- **What we learned after my last** ……….. Rage, Blip, Fury, Setback Aaaaaaaoutburst etc
- **They are** …………….. Slagging me off, gossiping about me, criticising, lying etc. This can be used as a visual flow chart to help people to decide ways of reacting when they feel 'got at'.
- **Rules For Life A** worksheet as described on page 240.
- **Who is in charge?** You or your anger

WIND-UP SCALE

Name: Week commencing:

	MON	TUE	WED	THU	FRI	SAT	SUN
MORNING							
AFTERNOON							
EVENING							

RECORD OF EMOTIONS

Name: Week commencing:

	MON	TUE	WED	THU	FRI	SAT	SUN
MORNING							
AFTERNOON							
EVENING							

ANGER DIARY

Date	What made you angry?	How angry did you feel? 0–100	Anger thermometer
			100 BOILING 90 80 BUBBLING 70 60 HOT 50 40 WARM 30 20 LUKE WARM 10 0 COOL

ANGER DIARY

What triggered the problem? What was happening before?	What did you do? What happened next?	What happened after that? How did you feel?

Filling out an anger diary?

Questions to ask

- When did your feeling of anger start?
- How angry did you feel? (Thermometer)
- How were you before that, were you calm?
- How did the day start? – was anything else happening on that day, or going on around you (environment or stress)?
- What was the trigger?
- What did you think about that? – did you have any thoughts at the time?
- How do you feel about the incident now?
- Do you feel that your reaction/behaviour made the situation any better/worse?

ANGER DIARY

Write down when you feel annoyed **or** lose your temper. Try to do this as soon as possible afterwards.

DATE	SITUATION	**FEELING:** How my body changed	**THOUGHT:** What I was thinking to myself	**BEHAVIOUR:** What I did

DIARY

Try to use this diary each time you experience strong feelings and/or thoughts (these could be positive or negative)

DATE	SITUATION/ EVENT	AUTOMATIC THOUGHTS ⊖	ALTERNATIVE THOUGHTS ⊕	FEELING (Bodily changes)	BEHAVIOUR
Wed	In pub or shop It was busy Stood in queue to be served A man was staring at me	Why is that guy staring at me? ⊖ Who the hell does he think he is? He deserves a 'bunch of fives'!	He doesn't know me – he's just interested in me or my clothes He's not a threat	Breathing faster Hot Heart racing Legs moving Hands tense	Stared back and glared at him
Fri	Sitting in TV room with George who keeps on about my clothes and the mess around my chair	He is always picking on me. ⊖ Leave me alone!	He doesn't always – usually he is my friend He often helps me	Gritting my teeth Breath heavier Stomach churns	Told him to 'p--- off!' Left the room and slammed the door!

DIARY

Try to use this diary each time you experience strong feelings and/or thoughts (these could be positive or negative)

DATE	SITUATION/ EVENT	AUTOMATIC THOUGHTS	ALTERNATIVE THOUGHTS	FEELING (Bodily changes)	BEHAVIOUR

THE TRAFFIC LIGHT ROUTINE

At the **first** sign of anger think of a set of traffic lights on red, so:

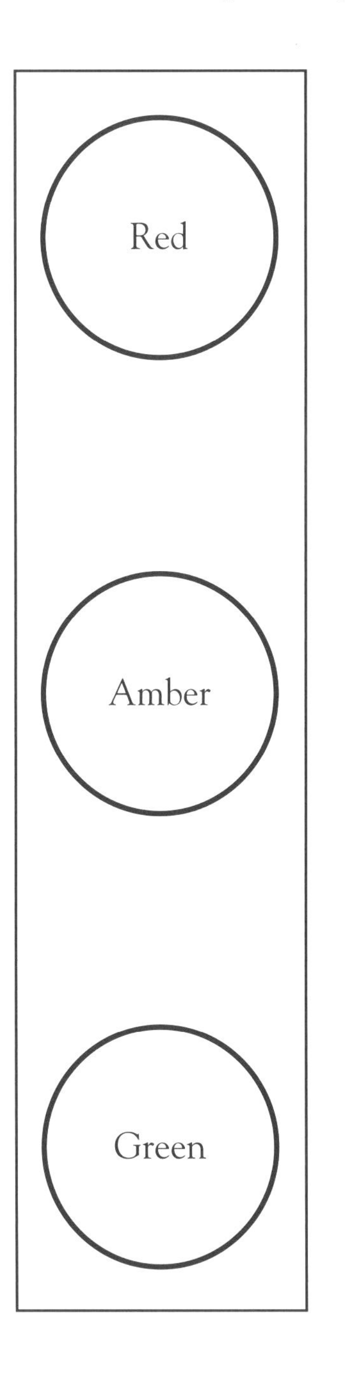

This sheet can be customised to the client's own wording

THE TRAFFIC LIGHT ROUTINE

At the **first** sign of anger think of a set of traffic lights on red, so:

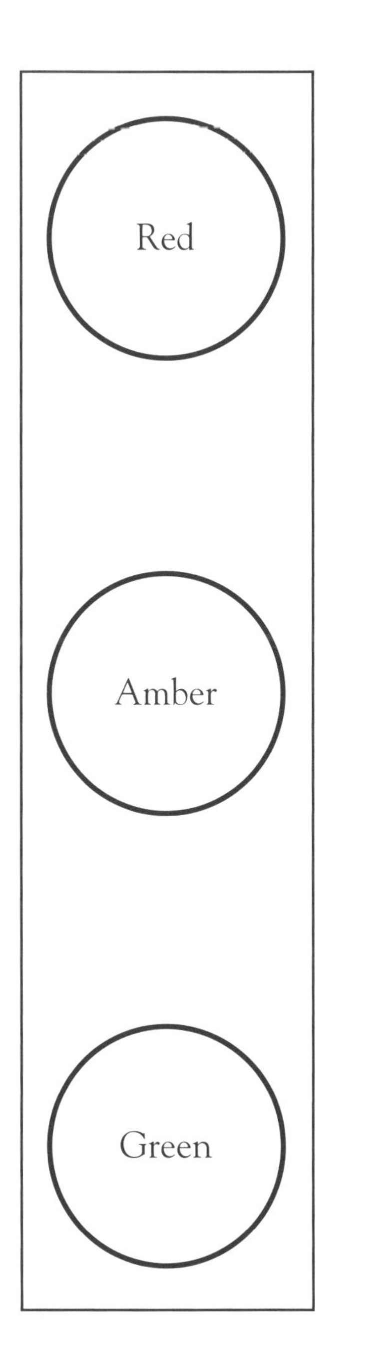

Shout out or imagine hearing the word
STOP!

GET READY – to calm down
Breathe out – blow away the anger
Stand still
Take two deep breaths

GO – move away
Take regular deep breaths
Use distraction techniques

THE TRAFFIC LIGHT ROUTINE

An example of a customised routine

At the **first** sign of anger think of a set of traffic lights on red, so:

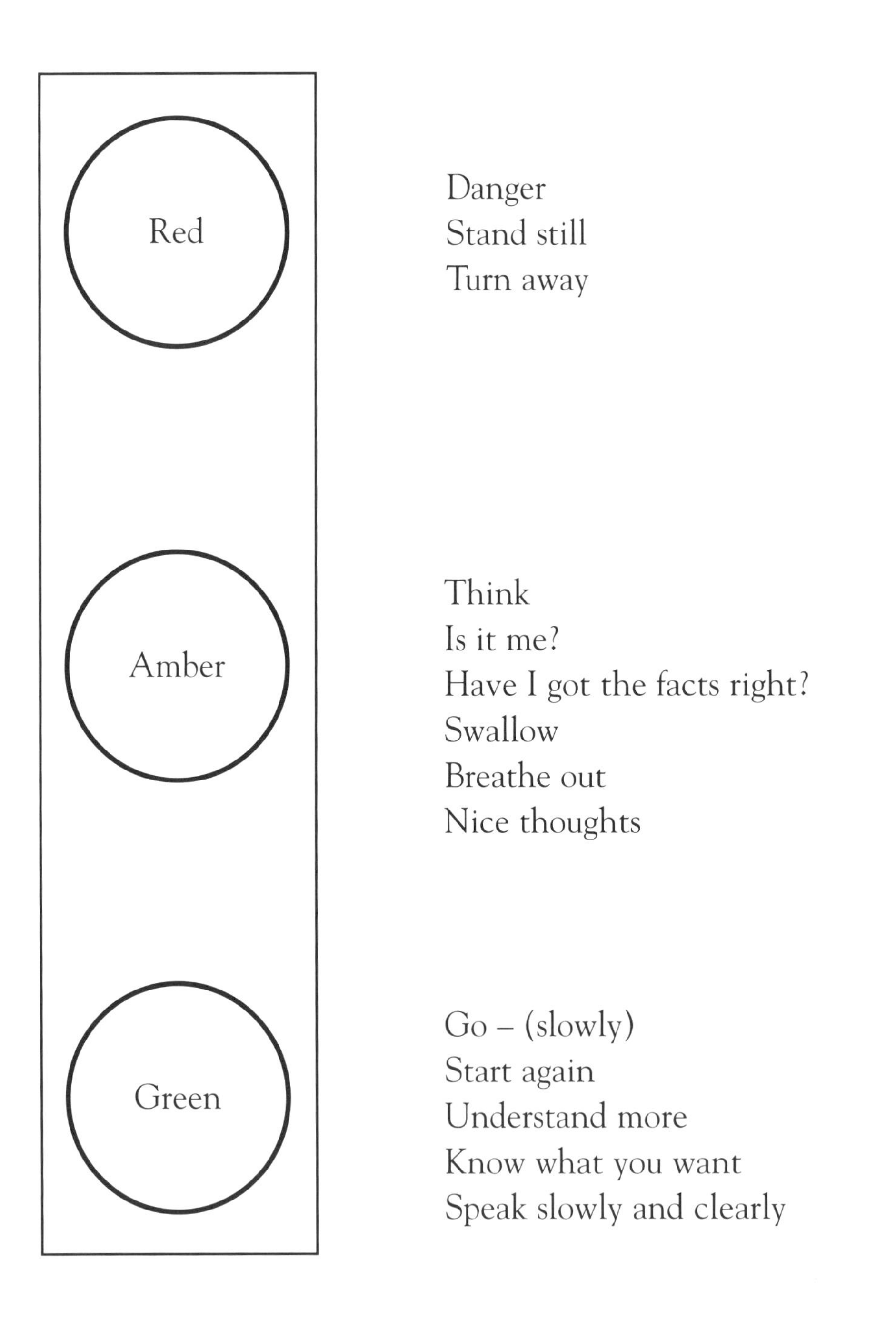

MANAGING ANGER

WAYS TO CALM YOUR

THOUGHTS	BODY	BEHAVIOUR
• Use self-instruction • Tell yourself you deserve to keep calm • Distraction • Count backwards • Imagery • Concentrate on something around you, e.g. the wallpaper, the clock-face, picture, etc. • Think of a funny picture • Traffic light sequence	• Arousal reduction • Breathe out first, then breathe in and out twice deeply • 10 slow breaths (count on fingers = interrupt anger sequence) • OTSAR • Use relaxation tape • Gentle rhythmical movement to music	• Move away separate from the others • Put hands by your side or in your pockets • Sit down in the chair, lean back and stretch those tense muscles • Change posture – stretch the body and 'break the tension' • Stretch out your arms, legs and fingers if sitting • Talk more slowly and quietly • Go for a walk • Listen to music • Swim • Exercise – remember to wind down at the end! • Get a cold drink • Find someone to talk to

MANAGING ANGER

WAYS TO CALM YOUR

THOUGHTS	BODY	BEHAVIOUR

Name ...Bill.................... Date ....

What we learned after my last rage ....

Positives	Things still to work on
I self-monitored well, and knew that it was best to stay on the ward and not go out.	But I did not tell anyone how bad I was feeling
I knew I was thinking a lot about what he called me, I was mulling it over. That was winding me up.	I could not think what to do to interrupt the process
I did eventually tell Annie that I needed help, well I asked her for some medication	Annie did not realise that I was so near the edge, so she said to have a quiet time and she would check on me in a while. Maybe I could (not should) have told her earlier and explained better
Then I went into the busy kitchen, I felt 'penned in' and my anger soared. But when Annie called me I did respond to her prompt to go outside	I know I need to stay out of the way of others when I'm wound up like that
I didn't hit anyone!	I still had an outburst in the courtyard – wish they hadn't all seen it
This is heaps better than I would have done in the past !	We have lots more to learn together!

Name ....

Date ....

What we learned after my last ....

Positives	**Things still to work on**

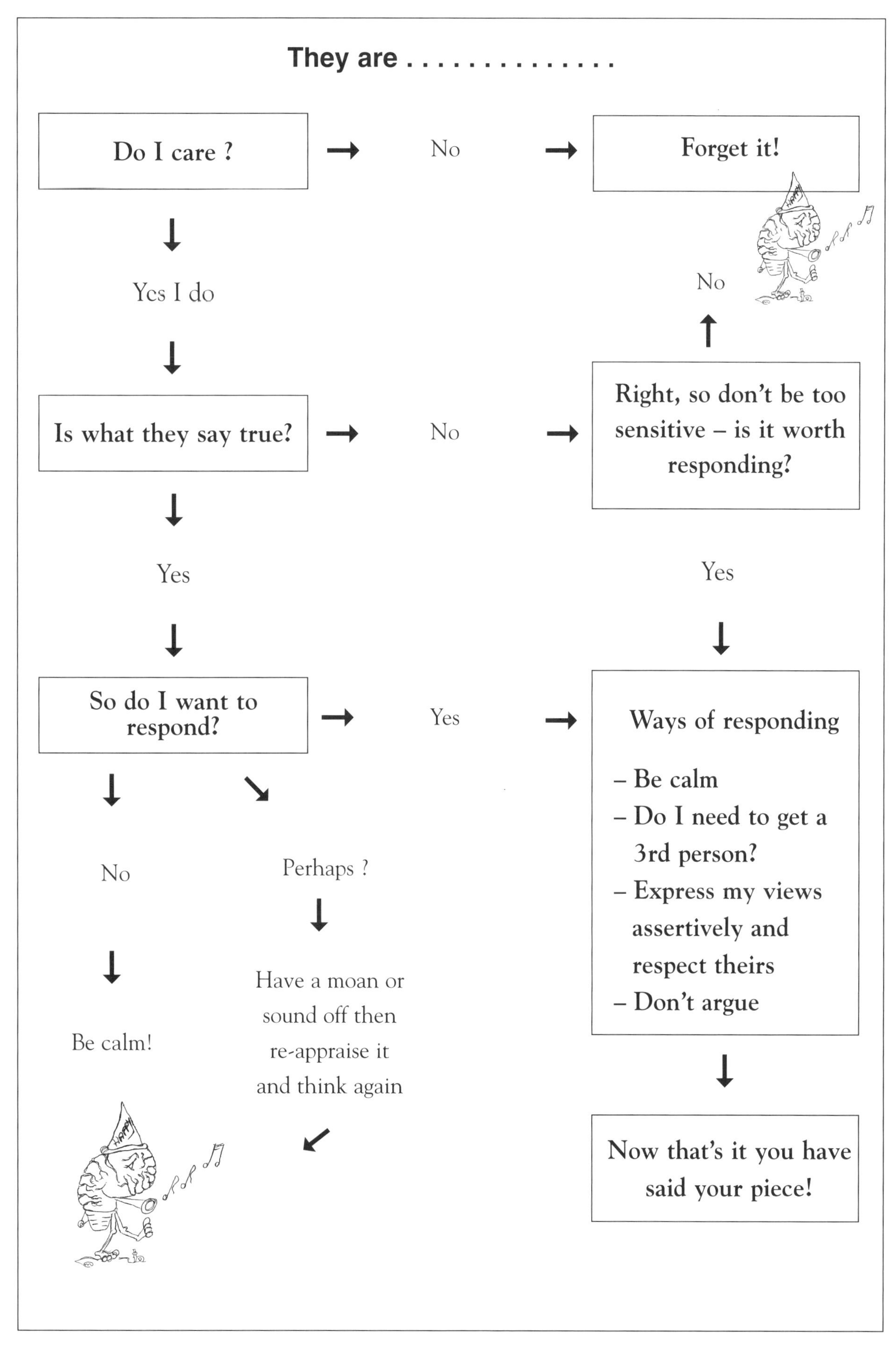
They are . . . .
Do I care ?
No
Forget it!
HAPPY
Yes I do
No
Is what they say true?
No
Right, so don't be too sensitive – is it worth responding?
Yes
Yes
So do I want to respond?
Yes
Ways of responding
– Be calm
– Do I need to get a 3rd person?
– Express my views assertively and respect theirs
– Don't argue
No
Perhaps ?
Have a moan or sound off then re-appraise it and think again
Be calm!
Now that's it you have said your piece!
HAPPY

RULE FOR LIFE WORKSHEET

RULE

Advantages	Disadvantages

So is this rule worth following, or is it a hindrance rather than a help?
Is the rule realistic? – Would other people try to follow it? – Ask them
Can you think of a replacement rule that might be less rigid and therefore kinder to you because it will not set you up for anger and frustration?

Who's in charge? – You or your anger?

Don't let your anger control you

Don't let your anger make you do things that you will later regret

So what can you do to take control?

Think or say – STOP ____________________

____

____

____

Remind yourself of your goals ____________________________

____

You deserve to be calm!

REFERENCES

If a reference is applicable to cognitive impairment the authors name is in **bold.**

Alderman N (2003) Contemporary approaches to the management of irritability and aggression following traumatic brain injury. Neuropsychological Rehabilitation 13: 211–40.

Alderman N, Ward A (1991) Behavioural treatment of the dysexecutive syndrome: reduction of repetitive speech using a response cost and cognitive overlearning. Neuropsychological Rehabilitation 1: 65–80.

Alderman N, Knight C, Henman C (2002) Aggressive behaviour observed within a neurobehavioural service: utility of OAS-MNR in clinical audit and applied research. Brain Injury 16: 469–89.

Alderman N, Knight C, Morgan C (1997) Use of a modified version of the Overt Aggression Scale in the measurement and assessment of aggressive behaviours following brain injury. Brain Injury 11: 503–23.

American Psychiatric Association (1994) Diagnostic and Statistical Manual of Mental Disorders IV. Washington, DC: APA.

Barratt E (1994) Impulsiveness and aggression. In Monahan J, Steadman H (Eds) Violence and Mental Disorder: developments in risk assessment. Chicago: University of Chicago.

Beck R, Fernandez E (1998) Cognitive-behavioural therapy in the treatment of anger: a meta-analysis. Cognitive Therapy and Research 22: 63–74.

Bellack A, Hersen M (1984) Research Methods in Clinical Psychology. New York: Pergamon Press.

Benson H (1976, 1985) The Relaxation Response, 6th edn. Glasgow: Collins.

Bernstein A (2003) How to Deal with Emotionally Explosive People. New York: McGraw-Hill.

Black L (1990) Treatment options for people with a mental handicap who are offenders. Issues in Criminology and Legal Psychology 16: 22–36.

Black L, Novaco RW (1993) Treatment of anger with a developmentally handicapped man. In Wells R, Giannetti V (Eds) Casebook of the Brief Psychotherapies. London: Plenum Press.

Black L, Cullen C, Novaco RW (1997) Anger assessment for people with mild learning disabilities in secure settings. In Kroese B, Dagnan D, Loumidis K (Eds) Cognitive-Behaviour Therapy for People with Learning Disabilities. London: Routledge.

Breakwell G (1989) Facing Physical Violence. London: B.P.S and Routledge.

Burns D (1990) The Feeling Good Handbook. New York: Plume.

Buss A, Perry M (1992) The aggression questionnaire. Journal of Personality and Social Psychology 63: 452–9.

Capara GV (1986) Indicators of Aggression: the dissipation-rumination scale. Personality and Individual Differences 7(6): 763–9.

Cornell D, Peterson C, Richards H (1999) Anger as a predictor of aggression among incarcerated adolescents. Journal of Consulting and Clinical Psychology 67: 108–15.

Davis D, Boster L (1992). Cognitive-Behavioural-Expressive intervention with aggressive and resistant youths. Child Welfare LXXI (6).

Denmark J, Gemeinhardt M (2002) Anger and its management for survivors of acquired brain injury. Brain Injury 16: 91–108.

Digiuseppe R (1995) Developing the therapeutic alliance with angry clients. In Kassinove H (Ed) Anger Disorders: definition, diagnosis and treatment. Bristol: Taylor & Francis.

Digiuseppe R, Tafrate R, Eckhardt C (1994) Critical Issues in the treatment of anger. Cognitive and Behavioural Practice 1: 111–32.

Dryden W (2000) Overcoming Anger. London: Sheldon Press.

D'Zurilla T, Goldfried M (1971). Problem solving and behaviour modification. Journal of Abnormal Psychology 78: 107–26.

Eames P, Wood R (2003) Episodic disorders of behaviour and affect after acquired brain injury. Neuropsychological Rehabilitation 13: 241–58.

Eckhardt C, Deffenbacher J (1995) In Kassinove H (Ed) Anger Disorders: definition, diagnosis and treatment. Bristol: Taylor & Francis.

Edmondson C, Conger J (1996) A review of treatment efficacy for individuals with anger problems: conceptual, assessment and methodological issues. Clinical Psychology Review 16: 251–75.

Ekman P (2003) Emotions Revealed: understanding faces and feelings. London: Phoenix.

Ellis A, Tafrate R (1997) How to Control your Anger before it Controls you. London: Robert Hale.

Feindler E (1991) Cognitive strategies in anger control interventions for children and adolescents. In Kendall PC (Ed) Child and Adolescent Therapy: Cognitive-behavioral procedures. New York: Guilford Press.

Feindler E (1995) Ideal treatment package for children and adolescents with anger disorders. In Kassinove H (Ed) Anger Disorders: definition, diagnosis and treatment. Bristol: Taylor & Francis.

Feindler E, Ecton R (1986) Adolescent Anger Control. New York: Pergamon Press.

Fleming J, Strong J, Ashton R (1996) Self-awareness in adults with traumatic brain injury: how best to measure? Brain Injury 10: 1–15.

Fogel BS (1994) The significance of frontal system disorders for medical practice and health policy. Journal of Neuropsychiatry 6: 343–47.

Gilmour K (1998) An anger management programme for adults with learning disabilities. International Journal of Language Communication Disorders 33: 402–8.

Golden C, Jackson M, Peterson-Rohne A, Gontkovsky S (1996) Neuropsychological correlates of violence and aggression: a review of the clinical literature. Journal of Aggression and Violent Behaviour 1: 3–25.

Goldstein A, Keller H (1987) Aggressive Behaviour: assessment and intervention. Oxford: Pergamon Press.

Hanks R, Temkin N, Machamer J, Dikmen S (1999). Emotional and behavioural adjustment after traumatic brain injury. Arch Phys Med Rehabilitation 80: 991–7.

Hartley L (1995) Cognitive-Communicative Abilities Following Brain Injury: a functional approach. London: Singular Publishing Ltd.

Headway Publication (2005) Managing Anger after a Brain Injury. Headway – the brain injury association.

Hilton N, Frankel A (2003) Therapeutic value of anger management programmes in a forensic setting. British Journal of Forensic Practice 5(2): 8–15.

Holland S, Ward C (2001) Assertiveness: a practical approach. Oxon: Winslow Press.

Howells K (1989) Anger management methods in relation to the prevention of violent behaviour. In Archer J. Browne K (Eds) Human Aggression: naturalistic approaches. London: Routledge.

Jacobson E (1938) Progressive Relaxation. Chicago: University of Chicago Press (Midway reprint, 1974).

Kellner M, Tutin J (1995) A school based anger management program for developmentally and emotionally disabled High School students. Adolescence 30(120): 813–25.

Kevan F (2003) Challenging behaviour and communication difficulties. British Journal of Learning Disabilities 31: 75–80.

Kim S, Manes F, Kosier T, Baruah S, Robinson R (1999). Irritability following traumatic brain injury. Journal of Nervous and Mental Disease 187: 327–35.

Kroese B, Dagnan D, Loumidis K (Eds) (1997) Cognitive-Behaviour Therapy for People with Learning Disabilities. London: Routledge.

LeDoux J (1996) The Emotional Brain. New York: Touchstone, Simon and Schuster.

Levey S, Howells K (1991) Anger and its management. Journal of Forensic Psychiatry 1: 305–27.

Liberman R, DeRisi W, Mueser K (1989). Social Skills Training for Psychiatric Patients. Boston: Allyn Bacon.

Lindsay W, Morrison F (1996) The effects of behavioural relaxation on cognitive performance in adults with severe intellectual disabilities. Journal of Intellectual Disability Research 40(4): 285–90.

Lindsay W, Overend H, Allan R, Williams C, Black L (1998) Using specific approaches for individual problems in the management of anger and aggression. British Journal of Learning Disabilities 26: 44–50.

Lochman J, Lenhart L (1993). Anger coping intervention for aggressive children: conceptual models and outcome effects. Clinical Psychology Review, 13: 785–805.

McDonald S, Flanagan S, Rollins S (2002) Awareness of Social Inference Test (TASIT). Oxford: Harcourt Assessment.

McDonnell A (1999) Defusing violent situations: low arousal approaches. British Journal of Therapy and Rehabilitation 16 (2).

McDonnell A, Reeves S, Johnson A, Lane A (1998) Managing challenging behaviour in an adult with learning disabilities: the use of a low arousal approach. Behavioual and Cognitive Psychotherapy 26: 163–71.

McKay M, Rogers P, McKay J (1989) When Anger Hurts: quieting the storm within. Oakland, CA: New Harbinger Press.

McMurran M, Charlesworth P, Duggan C, McCarthy L (2001) Controlling angry aggression: a pilot study with personality disordered offenders. Behavioural and Cognitive Psychotherapy 29: 473–85.

McNeil D, Eisner J, Binder R (2003) The relationship between aggressive attributional style and violence by psychiatric patients. Journal of Consulting and Clinical Psychology 71(2): 399–403.

Manchester D, Wood R (2001). Applying cognitive therapy in neurorehabilitation. In Wood R, Macmillan T (Eds) Neurobehavioral Disability and Social Handicap following Traumatic Brain Injury. Hove: Psychology Press.

Medd J, Tate R (2000) Evaluation of an Anger Management Therapy Programme following Acquired Brain Injury: a preliminary study. Neuropsychological Rehabilitation 10: 185–201.

Meichenbaum D (1975) A self-instructional approach to stress management: a proposal for stress inoculation. In Spielberger C, Sarason I (Eds) Stress and anxiety (vol 2) New York: Wiley.

Meichenbaum D (1985) Stress Inoculation Training. New York: Pergamon Press.

Meichenbaum D, Goodman J (1971) Training impulsive children to talk to themselves: a means of developing self-control. Journal of Abnormal Psychology 77: 113–26.

Miller R, Rollnick S (2002) Motivational Interviewing: preparing people to change (2nd edn) New York: Guilford Press.

Mitchell L (1977, 1987) Simple Relaxation: The Mitchell method for easing tension, 2nd edn. London: John Murray.

Morgan M. Hastings R (1998) Special Educators understanding of challenging behaviours in children with learning disabilities: sensitivity to information about behavioural function. Behavioural and Cognitive Psychotherapy 26: 43–53.

Murphy G, Clare I (1991) MIETS: a service option for people with mild mental handicaps and challenging behaviours or psychiatric problems. 2 Assessment, treatment, and outcome for service users and service effectiveness. Mental Handicap Research 4: 180–206.

Novaco RW (1978).Anger and coping with stress. In Foreyt JP, Rathjen D (Eds) Cognitive Behaviour Therapy. Lexington, MA: Heath.

Novaco RW (1988) Novaco provocation inventory. In Hersen M, Bellack A (Eds) Dictionary of Behavioural Assessment Techniques. New York: Pergamon Press.

Novaco RW (1992) A contextual perspective of anger with relevance to blood pressure In Johnson E, Gentry W, Julius S (Eds) Personality, Elevated Blood Pressure and Essential Hypertension. Washington: Hemisphere Publications.

Novaco RW (1993) Clinicians ought to view anger contextually. Behaviour Change 10: 208–18.

Novaco RW (1993–4) Stress Inoculation Treatment for Anger Control Therapist Procedures (1993–4 modifications). Available from Professor R. Novaco, University of California, Irvine, CA 92717, USA.

Novaco RW (1994a) Anger as a risk factor for violence among the mentally disordered. In Monahan J, Steadman H (Eds) Violence and Mental Disorder: developments in risk assessment. Chicago: University of Chicago Press.

Novaco RW (1994b) Clinical problems of anger and its assessment and regulation through a stress coping skills approach. In O'Donohue W, Krasner L (Eds) Handbook of Psychological Skill Training: clinical techniques and applications. Boston: Allyn & Bacon.

Novaco RW (1997) Remediating anger and aggression with violent offenders. Legal and Criminological Psychology 2: 77–88.

Novaco RW (2003) The Novaco Anger Scale and Provocation Inventory (NAS-PI). Los Angeles: Western Psychological Services.

Novaco RW, Ramm M, Black L (2000). Anger treatment with offenders. In Hollin C (Ed) Handbook of Offender Assessment and Treatment. London: John Wiley and Sons.

Novaco RW, Taylor J (2004). Assessment of anger and aggression in male offenders with developmental disabilities. Psychological Assessment 16: 42–50.

O'Callaghan M, Couvadelli B (1998) Use of self-instructional strategies with three neurologically impaired adults. Cognitive Therapy and Research 22: 91–107.

O'Neill H (1995) Anger: the assessment and treatment of problematic anger. British Journal of Occupational Therapy, 58: 427–31 and 469–72.

O'Neill H (1997) Relax, when I'm angry? You must be joking. Therapy Weekly, June 19.

O'Neill H (2002) Cognitive, cognitive what? British Journal of Occupational Therapy 65(6): 288–90.

Paterson B, Leadbetter D, McComish A (1997) De-escalation in the management of aggression and violence. Nursing Times 93: 58–61.

Payne RA (2000) Relaxation Techniques: a practical handbook for the health care professional. London; Churchill Livingstone.

Ponsford J, Sloan S, Snow P (1995) Traumatic Brain Injury: rehabilitation for everyday adaptive living. Hove: Lawrence Erlbaum Associates.

Pope S, Jones R (1996) The therapeutic effect of reactive self-monitoring on the reduction of inappropriate social and stereotypic behaviours. British Journal of Clinical Psychology 35: 585–94.

Poppen R (1989) Behavioural Relaxation Training and Assessment. Oxford: Pergamon Press.

Powell T (1992, 2001) The Mental Health handbook. Oxford, Winslow Press.

Powell T (2004) Head Injury: a practical guide. Oxon: Speechmark Publishing.

Prochaska J, DiClemente C (1982) Transtheoretical therapy: towards a more integrative model of change. Psychotherapy: Theory Research and Practice, 20: 161–73.

Prochaska J, DiClemente C, Norcross J (1992) In search of how people change: applications to addictive behaviours. American Psychologist 47: 1102–14.

Renwick S, Black L, Ramm M, Novaco R (1997) Anger treatment with forensic hospital patients. Legal and Criminal Psychology 2: 103–16.

Rose J, West C, Clifford D (2000) Group interventions for anger in people with intellectual disabilities. Research in Developmental Disabilities 21: 171–81.

Rosenberg M (1965) Society and the Adolescent Self-image. Princetown: Princetown University Press. This measure is available fom NFER-NELSON Publishing Company Ltd, Darville House, 2 Oxford Road East, Windsor, Berkshire SL4 1DF.

Schilling D, Poppen R (1983) Behavioural relaxation training. Journal of Behaviour Therapy and Experimental Research 14: 99–107.

Shammi P, Stuss D (1999) Humour appreciation: a role of the right frontal lobe. Brain 122: 657–66.

Siddle R, Jones F, Awenat F (2003) Group cognitive behaviour therapy for anger: a pilot study. Behavioural and Cognitive Psychotherapy 31: 69–83.

Spielberger C (1988) Manual for the State Trait Anger Expression Inventory. Odessa, FL: Psychological Assessment Resources.

Stallard P (2002) Think Good, Feel Good: a cognitive behaviour workbook for children and young people. Chichester: Wiley.

Stenfert Kroese B (1997) Cognitive-behaviour therapy for people with learning disabilities: conceptual and contextual issues. In Stenfert Kroese B, Dagnan D, Loumidis D (Eds) Cognitive-behaviour Therapy for People with Learning Disabilities. London: Routledge.

Stevenson H (1997) 'Missed, Dissed and Pissed': making meaning of neighbourhood risk, fear and anger management in urban black youth. Cultural Diversity and Mental Health: 3:37–52.

Sunderland M, Engleheart P (1994) Draw on Your Emotions. Oxford: Winslow Press.

Tafrate R (1995) Evaluation of treatment strategies for adult anger disorders. In Kassinove H (Ed) Anger Disorders: definition, diagnosis, and treatment. New York: Taylor & Francis.

Tanaka-Matsumi J (1995) Cross-cultural perspectives on anger. In Kassinove H (Ed) Anger Disorders: definition, diagnosis, and treatment. New York: Taylor & Francis.

Tavris C (1989) The Misunderstood Emotion, 2nd edn. New York: Touchstone.

Taylor J (2002) A review of the assessment and treatment of anger and aggression in offenders with intellectual disability. Journal of Intellectual Disability Research 46: 57–73.

Taylor J, DuQueno L, Novaco R (2004). Piloting award anger rating scale for older adults with mental health problems. Behavioural and Cognitive Psychotherapy 32: 467–79.

Taylor J, Novaco R (2005). Anger Treatment for people with developmental disabilities. Chichester: Wiley.

Taylor J, Novaco R, Gillmer B, Thorne I (2002) Cognitive-behavioural treatment of anger intensity among offenders with intellectual disabilities. Journal of Applied Research in Intellectual Disabilities 15: 151–65.

Taylor J, Novaco R, Gillmer B, Robertson A (2004) Treatment of anger and aggression. In Lindsay W, Taylor J, Sturmey P (Eds) Offenders with Developmental Disabilities. Chichester: Wiley.

Uomoto M, Brockway A (1992) Anger management training for brain injured patients and their family members. Archives of Physical and Medical Rehabilitation 73: 674–9.

Van Lancker D, Cummings J (1999) Expletives: neurolinguistic and neurobehavioral perspectives on swearing. Brain Research Reviews 31: 83–104.

Whitaker S (2001) Anger control for people with learning disabilities: a critical review. Behavioural Cognitive Psychotherapy 29: 277–93.

Wilcox D, Dowrick P (1992) Anger management with adolescents. Residential Treatment for Children and Youth. 9: 29–39.

Williams J (1990) Helping people to relax in over-stimulating environments. Mental Handicap 18: 160–2.

Williams H, Jones R (1997) Teaching cognitive self-regulation of independence and emotion control skills. In Kroese B, Dagnan D, Loumidis K (Eds) Cognitive-Behaviour Therapy for People with Learning Disabilities. London: Routledge.

Young A, Perrett D, Calder A, Sprengelmeyer R, Eckman P (2002) Facial Expressions of Emotion Simulation Test (FEEST): Oxford: Harcourt Assessment.

Zillman D (1983) Arousal and aggression. In Green RG, Donnerstein EI (Eds) Aggression: theoretical and empirical reviews. New York: Academic Press.

The Emotion Trainer is published by Media Innovations Ltd, 3 Gemini Business Park, Sheepscar Way, Leeds, LS7 3JB, UK and is now available to buy on PC CD-ROM.

A copy for parents or people who require a single user licence is available for £25 (plus VAT and postage). Please telephone +44 (0) 113 2849221 or +44 (0)113 262 1600 or Fax +44 (0) 113 2621605 or email for further information.

Relax – UK Ltd. On line resources for stress management and relaxation – Neuro biofeedback machine www.relax-uk.com

FURTHER READING

If a reference is applicable to cognitive impairment the author's name is in **bold**.

Averill JR (1983) Studies on anger and aggression. American Psychologist 11: 1145–60.

Crichton J (Ed) (1995) Psychiatric Patient Violence: risk and response. London: Duckworth.

Davis M, Robbins E, McKay M (2000) The Relaxation and Stress Reduction Workbook. USA: New Harbinger Publications Inc.

Deffenbacher J (1996) Cognitive behavioural approaches to anger reduction. In Dobson K, Craig K (Eds) Advances in Cognitive Behavioural Therapy. London: Sage.

Deffenbacher J, McNamara K, Stark R (1990) A comparison of cognitive–behavioural and process-orientated group counseling for general anger reduction. Journal of Counseling and Development 69: 167–72.

Grogan G (1991) Anger management: a perspective for occupational therapy. Ocupational Therapy in Mental Health 11: 135–47 and 149–71.

Herst K, Gunn J (Eds) (1991) The Mentally Disordered Offender. London: Butterworth-Heinemann.

Kassinove H (1995) Anger Disorders: definition, diagnosis, and treatment. New York, Taylor & Francis.

Lidbetter S (1994) Cognitive approaches to anger management. Mental Health Nursing 14: 199–221.

Lysaght R, Bodenhamer E (1990) The use of relaxation training to enhance functional outcomes in adults with traumatic head injuries. American Journal of Occupational Therapy 44: 797–802.

Moore E, Adams E, Elsworth J, Lewis J (1997) An anger management group for people with a learning disability. British Journal of Learning Disabilities 25: 53–7.

Novaco RW (1979).The cognitive regulation of anger and stress. In Kendall P, Hollon S (Eds) Cognitive Behavioural Interventions. New York: Academic Press.

O'Neill H (1997) Anger management: is it a job for OTs? British Journal of Therapy and Rehabilitation 4: 352–3.

Reeder D (1991) Cognitive therapy of anger management: theoretical and practical considerations. Archives of Psychiatric Nursing 5: 147–50.

Reiss S, Rojahn J (1993) Joint occurrence of depression and aggression in children and adults with mental retardation. Journal of Intellectual Disability Research 37: 287–94.

Shepherd J (Ed) (1994) Violence in Health Care: a practical guide to coping with violence and caring for victims. London: Oxford University Press.

Taylor E (1988) Anger intervention. American Journal of Occupational Therapy 42:147–54.

Whitehouse A (1994) Applications of cognitive therapy with survivors of head injury. Journal of Cognitive Psychotherapy: An international quarterly. 8: 41–160.

Participant Feedback

We would like you to tell us what you thought about the anger management course. This will help us when planning future courses.

Please could you comment on the following:

1. What did you like about the course?

2. Can you now recognise the 'warning' signs of anger?

3. Did you mind using a diary?

4. Can you remember any coping techniques?

5. Do you use any of them?

6. Do you sometimes need a reminder? e.g. a prompt from someone

7. Do you feel the course has helped you to manage your anger?

8. Give your reasons.

9. Is there anything that needs changing?

10. Any other comments?

Thank you for completing this form.